LOGOS
LATIN

LOGOS
LATIN

Julie Garfield

Illustrated by Mark Beauchamp

Logos Press
LEADERS IN CLASSICAL CHRISTIAN EDUCATION

Published by Logos Press, a division of Canon Press
PO Box 8729, Moscow, ID 83843
800.488.2034 | www.logospressonline.com | www.canonpress.com

Julie Garfield, *Logos Latin 4: Student Workbook*
Copyright © 2017 by Julie Garfield

Illustrations by Mark Beauchamp
Copyright © 2017 by Logos Press

Cover design by James Engerbretson
Interior layout by Jessica Evans and Valerie Anne Bost
Printed in the United States of America.

Library of Congress Cataloging-in-Publication Data

[[forthcoming]]

13 14 15 16 17 18 19 20   10 9 8 7 6 5 4 3 2 1

Table of Contents

Unit 3

Unit 4

Unit 5

Unit 6

Unit 7

Unit 8

Unit 9

Activity Pages

Reference Pages

Glossary

Index

Introduction

Dear Latin Student,

Welcome to *Logos Latin, Book 4.*

At this stage of your journey you are ready to navigate Latin more independently. You will become more proficient at recognizing English derivatives relating to Latin vocabulary. Your expertise in tracing the derivative etymologies (word histories) will grow. Sentence translation will flow with greater ease as you more readily recognize relationships between nouns and verbs. Sentences will increase in complexity as you learn more about modifiers and prepositional phrases.

As you review familiar active voice verb tenses you will also learn corresponding passive voice verbs. You will learn a new verb family, the fourth conjugation. You will continue to practice using all five noun cases and will add the vocative case. You will discover new ways to ask questions in Latin. You will investigate Latin pronouns to a much greater degree than before. In each unit you will encounter a new use for the mysterious and sometimes confusing ablative case.

Each unit in LOGOS LATIN 4 contains a Roman myth for you to translate. Vocabulary and grammar learned in the unit will help to prepare you for work on the myth. There are activity pages to go with each word list.

As always, the study of Latin challenges you to work hard and consistently. You have grown in your ability to think, to focus on details, to make connections, and to ask good questions. When the Latin road becomes rocky, do not bury your head in the sand like an ostrich! Instead, continue to ask lots of good questions and look on the problems as opportunities to win the race and reach your goal.

Here's to a great finish of grammar school Latin!

Julie Garfield

Unit 1

1 List One

VOCABULARY

Memorize the following Latin words and their translations.

WORD	DERIVATIVE	TRANSLATION
1. amīcus, -ī, *m.*	_____	*friend*
2. deus, -ī, *m.*	_____	*god*
3. rēx, rēgis*, *m.*	_____	*king*
4. vir, -ī**, *m.*	_____	*man*
5. fēmina, -ae, *f.*	_____	*woman*
6. terra, -ae, *f.*	_____	*land, earth*
7. ignis, ignis*, *m.*	_____	*fire*
8. sōl, sōlis*, *m.*	_____	*sun*
9. saxum, -ī, *n.*	_____	*rock*
10. ferramentum, -ī, *n.*	_____	*iron tool*
11. creō, -āre, -āvī, -ātum	_____	*create*
12. dō, -āre, dedī, datum	_____	*give*
13. iuvō, -āre, iūvī, iūtum	_____	*help*

*   third declension nouns
**   Vir is a second declension noun.

14. dēmōnstrō, -āre, -āvī, -ātum   _____   *show, point out*

15. dēvōrō, -āre, -āvī, -ātum   _____   *devour, swallow*

16. renovō, -āre, -āvī, -ātum   _____   *renew*

17. habitō, -āre, -āvī, -ātum   _____   *live in, inhabit*

18. fabricō, -āre, -āvī, -ātum   _____   *form, make, forge*

19. arō, -āre, -āvī, -ātum   _____   *plow*

20. amō, -āre, -āvī, -ātum   _____   *love, like*

REVIEW WORDS

1. liberī, -ōrum, *m.*   children
2. Iūlius, -ī, *m.*   Julius
3. Iūlia, -ae, *f.*   Julia, sister of Julius
4. Claudius, -ī, *m.*   Claudius or Claude, friend of Julius
5. Claudia, -ae, *f.*   Claudia, sister of Claudius and friend of Julia
6. Saxum, -ī, *n.*   Saxum is a companion of the children

A. FIRST CONJUGATION VERBS:

In Latin, the verb is the most important ingredient in the sentence. Usually the verb should be translated before any other word in the sentence.

The verb shows or expresses *action* or *state of being* and can tell *person* (the subject pronoun), *number* (whether the subject is singular or plural), and *tense* (the time of the action). Person, number, and tense are all contained in the verb ending.

The main part of the verb, called the *stem*, contains the meaning. The stem also tells us what verb family (conjugation) the verb is from. Latin has four conjugations or verb families but for now we will only consider the 1st conjugation or "A" family.

Most verbs have four principal parts which should be memorized whenever new verbs are introduced. We will use *amō* (meaning *I love*) as an example:

1st part	2nd part	3rd part	4th part
amō	*amāre*	*amāvī*	*amātum*

The second principal part of the verb is also called the *infinitive*. When used as an infinitive the *-re* ending is translated as *to*, so *amāre* means *to love*. In order to find the *present stem* of the verb we must remove the *-re* ending from the *second principal part* or *infinitive*.

Remove the *-re* from *amāre*.   *Amā-* is the present stem.

Now we can add endings to the stem. Watch how the endings change the subject pronoun in person and number. We will be using endings from the present tense, which means the time of the verb action is *now*. When translating present tense verbs from Latin into English the five present tense helping verbs can also be used: *am, is, are, do, does.*

Person	Singular	Plural
1st	amō — *I love, am loving, do love*	amā**mus** — *we love, are loving, do love*
2nd	amā**s** — *you love, are loving, do love*	amā**tis** — *you (pl.) love, are loving, do love*
3rd	ama**t** — *he, she, it loves, is loving, does love*	ama**nt** — *they love, are loving, do love*

N.B. Notice that in *amō* (1st person singular) the *a* is dropped from the stem in first conjugation verbs.

We can further illustrate the relationship of the present stem to its endings by considering the Latin flower below. The first layer of petals contains the present tense endings which can be attached to any present verb stem from the first conjugation.* Write the present tense endings on the flower below.

Verb Stem

*This will also be true for present tense verb stems from second conjugation.

B. INFINITIVES

Translate the infinitives below. The first one is done as an example.

1. amāre   _to love_

2. habitāre   _____

3. dēmōnstrāre   _____

4. dēvorāre   _____

5. fabricāre   _____

6. creāre   _____

7. renovāre   _____

8. arāre   _____

9. dāre   _____

10. iuvāre   _____

C. FINDING THE PRESENT TENSE VERB STEM

Remove the infinitive ending to find the present tense verb stem and write the stem on the line. The first one is done as an example.

1. amāre   _ama-_ _____

2. habitāre   _____

3. dēmōnstrāre   _____

4. dēvorāre   _____

5. fabricāre   _____

6. creāre   _____

7. renovāre   _____

8. arāre   _____

9. dāre   _____

10. iuvāre   _____

D. TRANSLATE: LATIN TO ENGLISH

Translate the present tense verbs below, paying close attention to the verb endings.

1. amās   _____

2. habitat   _____

3. dēmōnstrant _____

4. dēvorāmus   _____

5. fabricātis   _____

6. creō   _____

E. TRANSLATE IN THREE WAYS

Study the example and then translate these present tense verbs in three different ways.

1. _renovant_   _they renew_____ ,   _they are renewing_____ ,   _they do renew_____

2. _arō_   _____ ,   _____ ,   _____

3. _dat_   _____ ,   _____ ,   _____

4. _iuvās_   _____ ,   _____ ,   _____

F. TRANSLATE: ENGLISH TO LATIN

Translate these verbs into Latin. Make your verb ending match the subject pronoun.

1. She is creating. _____

2. We show. _____

3. They do inhabit. _____

G. PASSIVE VOICE

So far we have been using verbs in the *active voice,* where the subject noun performs the action of the verb. In the *passive voice,* the subject noun is acted upon by someone or something else.

For instance, if we say *The dog wags his tail* the dog is obviously performing the action of wagging.

But if we say *The dog is wagged by his tail* the dog is no longer performing the action of the verb even though he is the subject noun. The second sentence is in the *passive voice.*

Present tense, passive voice, endings are as follows: *-r, -ris, -tur, -mur, -minī, -ntur.*

These passive endings are attached to the present stem of the verb.

It is easier to understand the meaning of the present passive endings if we use an example.

PASSIVE VOICE, FIRST CONJUGATION

amor — *I am loved*	amāmur — *we are loved*
amāris — *you are loved*	amāminī — *you (pl.) are loved*
amātur — *he, she, it is loved*	amantur — *they are loved*

Underline the present stem in the present passive example above. As with the active voice, the stem for first person singular is not complete.

Lesson One 9

H. PRACTICE

Translate the following passive voice verbs into English:

1. dēmōnstrāmur _____

2. dātur _____

3. iuvāris _____

4. creantur _____

5. renovor _____

6. amāminī _____

I. REVIEW

1. What does the verb show? _____

2. What three things can the verb tell? _____

3. What principal part of the verb is used to find the present tense verb stem? _____

_____

J. DERIVATIVE DIGGING:

Look up the English word *fabricate* in a dictionary and write the definition on the lines below:

fabricate _____

_____

_____

② Lesson Two

A. FIRST, SECOND & SECOND DECLENSION NEUTER NOUNS (NOMINATIVE CASE)

In English we determine the *function* (part of speech) of a noun by word order. The noun looks the same whether it is a subject, direct object, object of the preposition, etc. In Latin we must determine the function of the noun by its endings (called *case endings*).

There are five noun cases in Latin: *nominative, genitive, dative, accusative,* and *ablative.* In this lesson we will consider the nominative case, or the subject noun.

We also need to recognize nouns from different families, called *declensions.* The declension endings we will be using in this lesson are listed below. Notice that the top row of each declension is the nominative case. These endings will be used to denote the subject noun. The left column of each declension is singular and the right column is plural.

First Declension

Case	Singular	Plural
Nom.	a	ae
Gen.	ae	ārum
Dat.	ae	īs
Acc.	am	ās
Abl.	ā	īs

Second Declension

Case	Singular	Plural
Nom.	us	ī
Gen.	ī	ōrum
Dat.	ō	īs
Acc.	um	ōs
Abl.	ō	īs

Second Dec. Neuter

Case	Singular	Plural
Nom.	um	a
Gen.	ī	ōrum
Dat.	ō	īs
Acc.	um	a
Abl.	ō	īs

B. DECLENSION PRACTICE

Practice declining (adding case endings) to the nouns below. Remember to find the *base* of the noun by removing the genitive singular ending before declining the nouns. The *declension* or noun family is identified by its genitive singular ending.

> *Don't try to change the case*
> > *until you find the base.*
> *The genitive case*
> > *is the place to find the base.*
> *And I forgot to mention*
> > *it also shows declension!*

First Declension

Case	Singular	Plural
Nom.	fēmina	
Gen.	fēminae	
Dat.		
Acc.		
Abl.		

Second Declension

Case	Singular	Plural
Nom.	amīcus	
Gen.	amīcī	
Dat.		
Acc.		
Abl.		

Second Declension Neuter

Case	Singular	Plural
Nom.	saxum	
Gen.	saxī	
Dat.		
Acc.		
Abl.		

C. SENTENCE EXAMPLES

Fēmina amat.	The woman loves.	*Fēminae amant.*	The women love.
Amīcus iuvat.	The friend helps.	*Amīci iuvant.*	The friends help.
Saxum fabricat.	The rock forms.	*Saxa fabricant.*	The rocks form.

Sentences containing a subject noun and a verb are called *Pattern 1 sentences.*

Nota Bene: In Second Declension Neuter the nominative and accusative cases look the same. We will learn how to distinguish them later.

Lesson Two 13

D. TRANSLATION: LATIN TO ENGLISH

Translate the following sentences into English.

1. Deus creat. _____

2. Virī dant. _____

3. Ferramentum arat. _____

4. Fēminae dēvorant. _____

5. Amīcī amant. _____

E. TRANSLATION: ENGLISH TO LATIN

Label the subject noun and verb, then translate the following sentences into Latin.

1. The lands are renewing. _____

2. God gives. _____

3. The woman is loving. _____

4. The rocks show. _____

5. The man inhabits. _____

F. PASSIVE VOICE

Translate the following passive voice verbs in to English:

1. creantur _____

2. iuvor _____

3. dēmōnstrāmur _____

4. renovāris _____

5. fabricantur _____

6. dāminī _____

14 Lesson Two

Now translate these passive voice verbs into Latin:

1. You (pl.) are loved. _____

2. It is renewed. _____

3. They are helped. _____

4. We are given. _____

5. I am created. _____

6. You are shown. _____

G. REVIEW

Identify the *declensions* of the following nouns (*first, second, or second neuter*) by looking at their genitive singular endings.:

1. ferramentum, -ī _____

2. terra, -ae _____

3. amīcus, -ī _____

Translate the following Pattern 1 sentences:

1. Iuvant. _____

2. Fēminae iuvant. _____

3. In #1 above, where do you find the subject noun? _____

Translate the infinitive *dēmōnstrāre* _____

What is the present stem for *demonstrō, dēmōnstrāre*? _____

Lesson Two   15

H. ETYMOLOGY

The *etymology* of a word is a history of how that word traveled into modern English from its original language. About half of our English words come from Latin, perhaps traveling from Italy through France and England before finally arriving on our shores. In addition to giving definitions of words, your English dictionary can also tell you the word's etymology. Usually, the etymology appears between brackets like these: [ ]. Read the sample etymology given below.

fabricate- [ME. *fabricaten*<L. *fabricatus*, pp. of *fabricari*, to construct, build<*fabrica*; SEE FABRIC]*

Here is a link to an easy-to-use, free online etymology dictionary: http://www. etymonline.com.

---

*. David B. Guralink, ed., *Webster's New World Dictionary of the American Language* (Englewood Cliffs, NJ: Prentice Hall, 1970), s.v. "fabricate.".

VOCABULARY

Memorize the following Latin words and their translations.

WORD	DERIVATIVE	TRANSLATION
1. equus, -ī, *m.*	_____	*horse*
2. telum, -ī, *n.*	_____	*weapon*
3. īra, -ae, *f.*	_____	*anger*
4. vulturīus, -ī, *m.*	_____	*vulture*
5. iecur, iecoris*, *n.*	_____	*liver*
6. dōnum, -ī, *n.*	_____	*gift*
7. fax, facis*, *f.*	_____	*torch*
8. flamma, -ae, *f.*	_____	*flame*
9. currus, -ūs**, *m.*	_____	*chariot*
10. habeō, -ēre, -uī, -itum	_____	*have, hold*
11. ligō, -āre, -āvī, -ātum	_____	*tie or bind*
12. sedeō, -ēre, sēdī, sessum	_____	*sit*
13. agito, -āre, -āvī, -ātum	_____	*drive*

*third declension noun
**fourth declension noun

WORD	DERIVATIVE	TRANSLATION
14. ardeō, -ēre, arsī, arsum	_____	*burn, blaze*
15. videō, -ēre, vīdī, vīsum	_____	*see*
16. et (conj.)	_____	*and*
17. sed (conj.)	_____	*but*
18. quod (conj.)	_____	*because*
19. ad *(prep. with acc.)*	_____	*to, toward*
20. in *(prep. with abl.)*	_____	*in, on*

REVIEW LIST

1. ventus, -ī, *m.*   *wind*
2. ambulō, -āre, -āvī, -ātum   *walk*
3. moveō, -ēre, mōvī, mōtum   *move*
4. volō, -āre, -āvī, -ātum   *fly*
5. possum, posse, potui, -----   *be able*
6. ā, ab *(prep. with abl.)*   *from, away from*
7. dē *(prep. with abl.)*   *down from*
8. ē, ex *(prep. with abl.)*   *out of, from*

③ Lesson Three

A. SECOND CONJUGATION VERBS (IMPERFECT & FUTURE TENSES):

Until now we have only been using first conjugation verbs, those which contain an *-a* at the end of the present stem. Second conjugation uses the same verb endings as first conjugation; the only difference is that the present stem of second conjugation verbs ends in *-e*.

We find the present stem in exactly the same way as we did before, by going to the *second principal part* of the verb and removing the *-re* ending. Consider the verb: *videō, vidēre, vīdī, vīsum*. Remove the *-re* from *vidēre* and you have the present stem *vidē*.

In addition to giving us the present stem, the second principal part also functions as the *infinitive*.

The *-re* ending is translated as *to*. For example, *vidēre* means *to see*.

Study *videō* as it is conjugated in the present tense below:

PRESENT TENSE

videō — *I see, am seeing, do see*	vidēmus — *we see, are seeing, do see*
vidēs — *you see, are seeing, do see*	vidētis — *you (pl.) see, are seeing, do see*
videt — *he, she, it sees, is seeing, does see*	vident — *they see, are seeing, do see*

IMPERFECT AND FUTURE TENSES, FIRST AND SECOND CONJUGATION VERBS

We have already learned how to find the present verb stem of first and second conjugation verbs and we have added present tense endings *(-ō, -s, -t, -mus, -tis, -nt)* to the present stem. Now we will learn two more tenses which also use the present stem.

The imperfect tense is one of two past tenses in Latin and shows ongoing action in the past. For example, *She was teaching music* implies that she was teaching music over an extended period of time. We could also say, *She used to teach music*. Helping verbs for the imperfect are *was, were,* and *used to*.

Imperfect Tense Endings

-bam — *I was, used to*	-bāmus — *we were, used to*
-bās — *you were, used to*	-bātis — *you (pl.) were, used to*
-bat — *he, she, it was, used to*	-bant — *they were, used to*

Now let's add the imperfect endings to the present stems of *amō* (a first conjugation verb) and *videō* (a second conjugation verb):

amābam — *I was loving*	amābāmus — *we were loving*
amābās — *you were loving*	amābātis — *you (pl.) were loving*
amābat — *he, she, it was loving*	amābant — *they were loving*

vidēbam — *I was seeing*	vidēbāmus — *we were seeing*
vidēbās — *you were seeing*	vidēbātis — *you (pl.) were seeing*
vidēbat — *he, she, it was seeing*	vidēbant — *they were seeing*

The future tense shows an action that will happen in the future. *She will teach music when she grows up.* The helping verb for the future tense is *will*.

Future Tense Endings

-bō- *I will*	-bimus — *we will*
-bis — *you will*	-bitis — *you (pl.) will*
-bit — *he, she, it will*	-bunt — *they will*

The future endings are also added to the present stem.

amābō — *I will love*	amābimus — *we will love*
amābis — *you will love*	amābitis — *you (pl.) will love*
amābit — *he, she, it will love*	amābunt — *they will love*

vidēbō — *I will see*	vidēbimus — *we will see*
vidēbis — *you will see*	vidēbitis — *you (pl.) will see*
vidēbit — *he, she, it will see*	vidēbunt — *they will see*

Now fill in the present, imperfect, and future tense endings on the blank petals of the Latin flower below. There is a layer of petals for each tense.

Verb Stem

B. TRANSLATION: LATIN TO ENGLISH

Translate the following Pattern 1 sentences into English. Watch for present, imperfect, and future tense verb endings.

1. Deus vidēbit. _____

2. Iūlius et Iūlia agitābant. _____

3. Sedēbō. _____

4. Ligātis. _____

5. Habēbimus. _____

6. Ardēbam. _____

7. Iuvās. _____

8. Saxum sedet. _____

9. Tēla ardēbant. _____

10. Dēmōnstrābis. _____

C. TRANSLATION: ENGLISH TO LATIN

Translate the following sentences into Latin:

1. We were seeing. _____

2. You (pl.) were sitting. _____

3. The king does have. _____

4. The men and women will help. _____

5. Claudius was driving. _____

6. We are showing. _____

7. You were giving. _____

8. You (pl.) will bind. _____

9. The torch will burn. _____

10. The vultures were devouring. _____

D. PASSIVE VOICE

We have learned the present tense for first conjugation verbs in the passive voice. Now let's add the imperfect and future tenses. Note that second conjugation behaves like the first conjugation except for the "-e" at the end of the present stem. The present stem is used for the present, imperfect, and future passive endings. Study the examples of passive verbs below:

Imperfect Passive

amābar — *I was (being) loved*	amābāmur — *we were (being) loved*
amābāris — *you were (being) loved*	amābaminī — *you (pl.) were (being) loved*
amābātur — *he, she, it was (being) loved*	amābantur — *they were (being) loved*

Future Passive

vidēbor — *I will be seen*	vidēbimur — *we will be seen*
vidēberis — *you will be seen*	vidēbiminī — *you (pl.) will be seen*
vidēbitur — *he, she, it will be seen*	vidēbuntur — *they will be seen*

N.B. In the future passive, "be" must be there!

Lesson Three (23)

E. PASSIVE TRANSLATION: LATIN TO ENGLISH

Translate the following imperfect and future passive voice verbs or sentences containing those verbs into English. The first two are done for you.

1. Agitābāmur. _____We were driven._____

2. Equus dēvorābitur. __The horse will be devoured._____

3. Ligābuntur. _____

4. Fax vidēbātur. _____

5. Creābāminī. _____

6. Deus amābitur. _____

7. Renovābar. _____

8. Virī vidēbantur. _____

9. Sedēbimur. _____

10. Iuvābāris. _____

F. PASSIVE TRANSLATION: ENGLISH TO LATIN

Now translate the following English sentences containing the passive voice into Latin. Present, imperfect, and future tenses are used. The first two are done as examples

1. The gift was given.   *Donum dabātur.*

2. The gifts were held.   *Dona habēbantur.*

3. The iron tools will be forged. _____

4. We are being renewed. _____

5. I am seen. _____

6. The men were being bound. _____

7. You (pl.) were being helped. _____

8. The lands will be burned. _____

9. They are being seated._____

10. (His) friend was being driven._____

N.B. Possessive pronouns such as *his* in sentence #10 above are often implied. You do not have to translate *his*.

G. REVIEW

1. Name the five helping verbs for the *present tense.*_____

_____

2. How do you find the *present stem* of a first conjugation verb?

_____

_____

3. Translate the present tense verb *videt* in three ways.

_____

_____

_____

4. Make the following sentence plural in Latin: *Vir creat.*

_____

5. Name the four principal parts for the verb meaning *give.*

_____

H. TIDBIT

Mars, the Roman god of war, often had a dog or a vulture associated with him.

If you are able, consider checking out these links for more information:

- *kids.britannica.com/elementary/article-353433/Ares*
- *mensaforkids.org/teach/lesson-plans/an-introduction-to-greek-mythology*

(4) Lesson Four

A. ACCUSATIVE CASE (1ST, 2ND & 2ND DECLENSION NEUTER NOUNS):

So far we have only been dealing with Pattern 1 sentences or sentences which contain a subject noun and a verb. Now we will work with Pattern 2 sentences which also contain a *direct object*. The direct object is a noun which receives the action of the verb whereas the *subject noun* gives or does the action of the verb. Let's look at some English examples:

SN   V-t   DO

Example #1:   *Julius drives the horse.*

In this sentence *Julius* is the subject noun, *drives* is the verb, and *horse* is the direct object.

Now let's rearrange the nouns:

SN   V-t DO

Example #2:   *The horse drives Julius.*

Horse becomes the subject noun and *Julius* becomes the direct object.

In English, word order determines the *function (or part of speech)* of a noun. In Latin, *function* is determined by the case ending. We already know that the nominative ending denotes a subject noun. To show that a noun is a direct object we must use the *accusative* ending.

Let's translate our first example from above into Latin.

SN   DO   V-t
Iūlius equum agitat.

Notice that *Iūlius* as the subject noun is in the nominative case for second declension.

Equum, also a second declension noun, is in the accusative case because it is the direct object.

Now look at the translation of the second example from above:

SN   DO   V-t
Equus Iūlium agitat.

The word *horse* is put in the nominative case to become the subject noun while the name *Iūlius* is put in the accusative case as the direct object. Usually the direct object precedes the verb in a Latin sentence .

Review the nominative and accusative case endings for *first, second, and second declension neuter* on your charts before beginning this lesson. **N.B.** Verbs which take a direct object are called *transitive verbs*. The abbreviation for a transitive verb is *v-t*.

B. TRANSLATION: LATIN TO ENGLISH

Label and translate the following Pattern 2 sentences into English.

Direct objects will be labeled *DO* and verbs in Pattern 2 sentences will be labeled *V-t*.

1. Vir ferramentum fabricat. _____

_____

2. Iūlius et Claudius terram arābant. _____

_____

3. Iūlia et Claudia fēminās iuvābunt. _____

_____

4. Habēmus equum. _____

_____

5. Fabricābitis tēla. _____

_____

6. Flammae terrās dēvorant. _____

_____

7. Deus virōs et fēminās creābat._____

_____

8. Dābō dōnum._____

_____

9. Liberī tēla vident. _____

_____

10. Deī iram habēbunt. _____

_____

C. TRANSLATION: ENGLISH TO LATIN

Label and translate the following Pattern 2 sentences into Latin:

1. The king will like the gift._____

_____

_____

2. The man makes a weapon. _____

_____

3. The women point out the rocks. _____

_____

4. The vultures will devour the horse._____

_____

5. God was helping a man. _____

_____

D. PASSIVE VOICE: TRANSLATION

Practice translating the following passive voice verbs from the *present, imperfect,* and *future tenses* into English:

1. Creābar. _____

2. Iuvābitur. _____

3. Fēminae sedēbuntur. _____

4. Dōnum dātur. _____

5. Renovābāmur. _____

6. Vidēminī. _____

7. Amor. _____

8. Equus dēmonstrābātur. _____

9. Ardebāntur. _____

10. Amābiminī. _____

Translate these passive voice verbs into Latin:

1. We will be renewed. _____

2. The horses were being shown. _____

3. The flames are seen. _____

4. I will be helped. _____

*Challe*nge: You are given a gift. _____

E. REVIEW

1. What case is used for the subject noun? _____

2. What case is used for the direct object? _____

3. What is the present tense verb stem for *habito*? _____

4. What are the helping verbs for the present tense? _____

5. What are the helping verbs for the imperfect tense? _____

6. What is the helping verb for the future tense? _____

5 Lesson Five

A. ABLATIVE OF PLACE WHERE & ABLATIVE OF PLACE FROM WHICH

WHERE:

The ablative case can be used with the preposition *in* to show *where* something occurs.

Study the examples below:

in equō	on the horse, in the horse
in terrā	in the land, on the land
in saxō	on the rock, in the rock

FROM WHICH:

The ablative case can also be used with the prepositions *ā, ab (from, away from), ē, ex (out of, from),*

or *dē (down from)* to show the place from which movement occurs. For example:

Vir ab equō movēbat.	The man was moving *away from the horse.*
Fēmina ē terrā ambulābit.	The woman will walk *out of the land.*
Vulturius dē saxō volat.	The vulture is flying *down from the rock.*

B. TRANSLATION: LATIN TO ENGLISH

Label and translate these sentences.

1. Vir ferramenta fabricābat.

_____

2. Līberī et Saxum in terrā sedēbant et virum spectābant. _____

_____

3. Vir ā tēlō movēbat. _____

4. Iūlius et amīcus tēla habent. _____

5. Claudius tēlum creābit. _____

6. Iūlia et Claudia virum iuvant ferramenta fabricāre. _____

_____

7. Ferramentum terram arābit. _____

C. PASSIVE TRANSLATION: LATIN TO ENGLISH

Translate these sentences containing passive verbs.

1. Terra ardēbātur.   _____

2. Fēminae iuvābuntur.   _____

3. Tēlum dēmōnstrābitur.   _____

4. Vidēmur.   _____

5. Dōnum dābātur.   _____

6. Vir creātur.   _____

7. Renovāminī.   _____

D. *POSSUM* REVIEW

Study the possum chant and meanings below.

possum — *I am able*	possumus — *we are able*
potes — *you are able*	potestis — *you (pl.) are able*
potest — *he, she, it is able*	possunt — *they are able*

Forms of the verb *possum* are often followed by an infinitive to complete the meaning. Study the example and translate the sentences below containing this verb in combination with infinitives.

1. Possum terram arāre.   *I am able to plow the land.* _____

2. Iūlius potest currum agitāre._____

_____

3. Līberī et Saxum possunt ferramenta fabricāre. _____

_____

4. Potestis vulturīum vidēre in saxō. _____

_____

6 Lesson Six
How Fire Came to Man

Translate the story of Prometheus.

1. Promētheus ante hominibus in terrā habitābat. _____

_____

2. Deī Promētheum iubēbant hominēs creāre. _____

_____

3. Promētheus ex aquā et terrā hominēs formābat. _____

_____

4. Sed Promētheus dōnum nōn habuit. _____

_____

5. Minerva Promētheum iuvābat. _____

_____

6. Dea Promētheum volāre ad sōlem iuvābat. _____

_____

7. Iuppiter Promētheum dicit, "Nōn potes hominibus ignem dāre." _____

_____

8. Sed Promētheus facem in currū sōlis ponēbat et flammās ad terram portābat. _____

_____

_____

9. Ignis hominēs iuvābat ferramenta et tēla fabricāre. _____

_____

10. Virī poterant bella pugnāre et terram arāre. _____

_____

11. Promētheus virōs iuvābat sed Iuppiter, rēx deōrum, īram habēbat. _____

_____

_____

12. Iuppiter Promethēum ligābat ad saxum. _____

_____

13. Vulturīus iēcur dēvorābat sed iēcur renovābātur cotidiē. _____

_____

14. Postrēmō, Hercules Promētheum liberāvit. _____

_____

GLOSSARY

1. ante *(prep. w/abl.)*   *before*
2. aqua, -ae, f.   *water*
3. bellum, -ī, n.   *war*
4. cotidiē   *every day*
5. dea, -ae, f.   *goddess*
6. dicit   *he, she, it tells*
7. formō, -āre, -āvī, -ātum   *form, shape, fashion*
8. homō, hominis m.   *man (in the sense of human being)*
9. iubeō, iubēre, iussī, iussum   *order, command*
10. liberāvit   *he, she, it freed*
11. liberō, -āre, -āvī, -ātum   *set free*
12. Minerva, -ae, f.   *goddess of wisdom*

13. nōn habuit — *did not have*

14. pōnō, pōnere, posuī, positum — *put, place*

15. portō, -āre, -āvī, -ātum — *carry*

16. possum, posse, potuī, ---------- — *be able*

17. postrēmō — *finally*

18. poterant — *they were able*

19. pugnō, -āre, -āvī, -ātum — *fight*

20. rēx deōrum — *king of the gods*

21. rogō, -āre, -āvī, -ātum — *ask*

22. sōl, sōlis m. — *sun*

23. ventus, -ī m. — *wind*

24. volō, -āre, -āvī, -ātum — *fly*

Unit One Review

A. PRINCIPAL PARTS

Write out the four principal parts for the following verbs:

VERB	1ST	2ND	3RD	4TH
1. create	_____	_____	_____	_____
2. give	_____	_____	_____	_____
3. help	_____	_____	_____	_____
4. sit	_____	_____	_____	_____
5. see	_____	_____	_____	_____
6. have, hold	_____	_____	_____	_____

B. CONJUGATIONS

Give the present tense verb stem for the following verbs and tell what *conjugation (verb family)* each is from.

VERB	PRESENT STEM	CONJUGATION
1. renovō	_____	_____
2. ardeō	_____	_____

C. ACTIVE VERBS

Translate the *active voice* verbs below.

1. habēbat   _____

2. dēvorābimus   _____

3. sedeō   _____

4. dēmōnstrās   _____

5. fabricābit   _____

6. arābant   _____

D. PASSIVE VERBS

Now translate these *passive voice* verbs:

1. habēbātur   _____

2. devorābimur   _____

3. sedeor   _____

4. dēmōnstrāris   _____

5. fabricābitur   _____

6. arābantur   _____

E. TRANSLATION: LATIN TO ENGLISH

Translate the sentences below.

1. Vir terram habitābat. _____

_____

2. Rēx iram habet. _____

3. Rēx vīrum ad saxum ligat. _____

4. Ignis terram ardēbat. _____

5. Ventus flammās ad virum agitābat. _____

_____

6. Amīcī flammās vident et virum iuvant. _____

_____

F. DERIVATIVE PRACTICE

Use ten derivatives from Lists 1 and 2 in a short story. Use an English dictionary to help you with any words you do not understand. Underline the derivatives used.

_____

_____

_____

_____

_____

_____

_____

_____

_____

_____

_____

Unit 2

3 List Three

VOCABULARY

Memorize the following vocabulary words, including the genitives and genders for nouns and the four principal parts for verbs.

WORD	DERIVATIVE	TRANSLATION
1. fābula, -ae, *f.*	_____	*story, legend*
2. poena, -ae, *f.*	_____	*penalty, punishment*
3. caelum, -ī, *n.*	_____	*sky, heaven*
4. forma, -ae, *f.*	_____	*shape, beauty*
5. mūsica, -ae, *f.*	_____	*music*
6. frāter, frātris*, *m.*	_____	*brother*
7. vōx, vōcis, *f**	_____	*voice*
8. avāritia, -ae, *f.*	_____	*greed*
9. invidia, -ae, *f.*	_____	*envy*
10. cūra, -ae, *f.*	_____	*care, worry*
11. morbus, -ī, *m.*	_____	*sickness, disease*
12. spēs, -eī**, *f.*	_____	*hope*
13. malevolentia, -ae, *f.*	_____	*spite, malice*

*third declension nouns
**fifth declension noun

14. benevolentia, -ae, *f.* _____ *goodwill, kindness*

15. possum, posse, potuī, ----- _____ *be able*

16. apportō, -āre, -avī, -ātum _____ *bring*

17. moneō, -ēre, monuī, monitum _____ *warn*

18. levō, -āre, -avī, -ātum _____ *lift*

19. dē *(prep. with abl.)* _____ *about, concerning, down from, from*

20. contrā *(prep. with abl.)* _____ *against*

REVIEW WORDS

1. narrō, -āre, -avī, -ātum   *tell*
2. amīcus, -ī, *m.*   *friend*
3. auscultō, -āre, -āvī, -ātum   *listen to*
4. portō, -āre, -āvī, -ātum   *carry*
5. Aesōpus, Aesōpī, *m.*   *Aesop*

7 Lesson Seven

A. PERFECT TENSE (FIRST & SECOND CONJUGATION VERBS):

We have learned the present, imperfect, and future tense endings which are attached to the *present stem*. We know that the present stem is formed from the *second principal part (or infinitive)* of the verb. We also know that the *imperfect tense* is a past tense used to talk about something which occurred over a period of time in the past. For example, "The Founding Fathers were writing the United States Constitution for months."

The *perfect tense* is also a past tense but it is used to talk about an action in the past which is "over and done with," instead of one occurring over a period of time. If we say, "The Founding Fathers signed the Declaration of Independence on July 4, 1776," that is an example of the perfect tense. It is a specific action in the past which has been completed.

Now we will learn the *perfect tense verb endings*. These endings are added to a different stem called the *perfect tense verb stem*. The perfect stem is formed by removing the ending from the third principal part of the verb. In English, these endings can be translated by simply adding *-ed* to the verb or by using the helping verbs *has, have,* or *did*.

ī — *I -ed, have, did*	imus — *we -ed, have, did*
istī — *you -ed, have, did*	istis — *you (pl.). -ed, have, did*
it — *he, she, it -ed, has, did*	ērunt — *they -ed, have, did*

The perfect stem is formed by removing the *-ī* from the third principal part of the verb. For example:

> *portō, portāre, portāvī, portātum*

Remove the *-ī* from *portāvī* and the perfect stem is *portāv-* . Let's add the perfect tense endings to the perfect stem and translate:

portāvī — *I carried, have carried, did carry*	portāvimus — *we carried, have carried, did carry*
portāvistī — *you carried, have carried, did carry*	portāvistis — *you (pl.) carried, have carried, did carry*
portāvit — *he, she, it carried, has carried, did carry*	portāvērunt — *they carried, have carried, did carry*

Now consider an example from second conjugation: *moneō, monēre, monuī, monitum*

Again, remove the *-ī* from *monuī*, and the perfect stem *monu-* remains.

monuī — *I warned, have warned, did warn*	monuimus — *we warned, have warned, did warn*
monuistī — *you warned, have warned, did warn*	monuistis — *you (pl.) warned, have warned, did warn*
monuit — *he, she, it warned, has warned, did warn*	monuērunt — *they warned, have warned, did warn*

Study the perfect stem Latin flower:

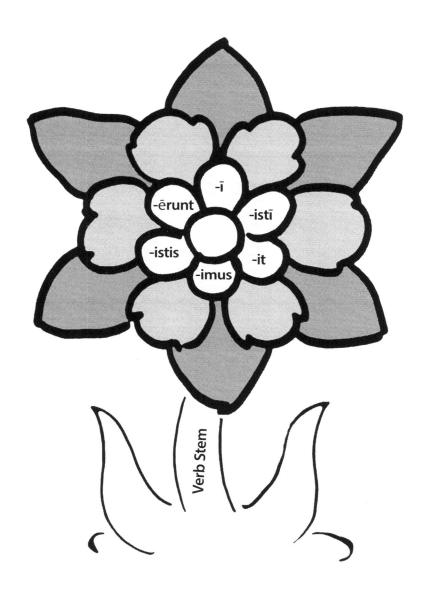

B. PERFECT TENSE

Translate the following sentences containing perfect tense verbs into English.

1. Creāvērunt. _____

2. Levāvistī. _____

3. Dedit. _____

4. Apportāvimus. _____

5. Monuī. _____

6. Vīdistis. _____

7. Līberī fabulās narrāvērunt dē equīs. _____

_____

8. Iūlia dōnum dedit. _____

9. Claudius et Iūlius morbum habuērunt. _____

_____

10. Saxum mūsicam amāvit. _____

_____

C. TRANSLATION: ENGLISH TO LATIN

Label and translate the following sentences into Latin. Many contain verbs in the perfect tense.

1. Prometheus brought flames to the earth.

_____

_____

_____

Lesson Seven   51

2. Julia told a story about the gods. _____

_____

3. Jupiter has given a punishment. _____

_____

4. Men and women did have greed and envy . _____

_____

5. But hope will bring kindness. _____

D. PASSIVE VOICE REVIEW

Translate the passive verbs below into Latin. All are from the present, imperfect, and future passive tenses.

1. He was warned.   _____

2. It will be brought.   _____

3. They are carried.   _____

4. The story will be told. _____

5. We were lifted.   _____

E. REVIEW

1. Conjugate and translate *dēmōnstrō* in the imperfect tense, active voice:

2. What is the present stem of *creō*? _____

3. What case is used for *subject nouns*? _____

4. What case is used for *direct objects*? _____

5. Conjugate and translate *portō* in the imperfect tense, *passive voice*.

F. DERIVATIVE

Choose a derivative from List 3 that you don't know well. Look it up in an English dictionary and write the definition below. Then use the derivative in a creative sentence that shows its meaning.

Derivative: _____

Definition: _____

_____

Sentence: _____

_____

8 Lesson Eight

A. GENITIVE CASE (1ST, 2ND & 2ND DECLENSION NEUTER NOUNS)

The genitive case endings are used to show possession in Latin. In English, we use *-'s, -s'*, or the preposition *of* to show ownership. Notice that in Latin the possessive noun frequently follows the noun it describes. In fact, we can consider it a type of adjective and can label it PNA (possessive noun adjective). Now compare singular and plural possessive nouns in first, second, and second neuter declensions. The genitive words appear in bold type. Underline or highlight the genitive endings on the Latin possessive nouns.

1st Dec. Singular	the girl's gift, the gift of the girl	*dōnum* **puellae**
1st Dec. Plural	the girls' gift, the gift of the girls	*dōnum* **puellārum**
2nd Dec. Singular	the friend's music, the music of the friend	*mūsica* **amīcī**
2nd Dec. Plural	the friends' music, the music of the friends	*mūsica* **amīcōrum**
2nd Dec. N. Singular	the sky's beauty, the beauty of the sky	*forma* **caelī**
2nd Dec. N. Plural	the skies' beauty, the beauty of the skies	*forma* **caelōrum**

B. TRANSLATION: LATIN TO ENGLISH

Translate the following sentences. Many contain nouns in the gentive case.

1. Līberī amant fābulās Aesōpī auscultāre. _____

_____

2. Frāter Claudiae fābulam dē avāritiā narrāvit. _____

_____

3. Saxum fābulam dē deīs ēt deabus* narrāvit. _____

_____

4. Rēx deōrum contrā Promētheum malevolentiam habuit in fābulā Saxī. _____

_____

5. Līberī mūsicam fēminārum auscultāvērunt. _____

_____

* *Deabus* is the abl. plural form of *dea*, "goddess".

C. TRANSLATION: ENGLISH TO LATIN

Translate the following phrases into Latin. Use only the nominative and genitive cases.

1. God's heaven   _____

2. woman's beauty   _____

3. the women's envy   _____

4. the horses' land   _____

5. the sky's sun   _____

6. the man's greed   _____

D. REVIEW

Translate the active and passive voice verbs below from the present, imperfect, and future tenses.

1. creābam   _____

   creābār   _____

2. levābis   _____

   levābēris   _____

3. portat   _____

   portātur   _____

4. sedēmus   _____

   sedēmur   _____

5. renovābitis   _____

   renovābiminī   _____

6. monēbant   _____

   monēbantur   _____

E. ETYMOLOGY

Look up the etymology for the word *envy* and write it on the lines below.

N.B. The etymology is the history of the derivative, not the meaning. The etymology will appear in brackets. This symbol, <, means *comes from*. Ssome dictionaries use the abbreviation *fr.* (from).

_____

_____

_____

_____

Consider the etymology of *wise*. Notice the surprising connections back to this word's Latin origin.

[ME *wis* < OE, akin to *witan*, to know < PGmc *wisa-*, wise < IE base *weid-*, to see, know, whence Sans *vedas*, knowledge, Gr *idris*, knowing, L. *videre*, to see]**

Explanation of the etymology of *wise*: Middle English from Old English, related to *witan*, to know, from Primitive Germanic *wisa-*, meaning wise from Indo-European base *weid-*, meaning to see or know, whence Sanskrit *vedas* meaning knowledge, Greek *idris* meaning knowing, Latin *videre* meaning to see.

** David B. Guralink, ed., *Webster's New World Dictionary of the American Language* (Englewood Cliffs, NJ: Prentice Hall, 1970), s.v. "wise."

4 List Four

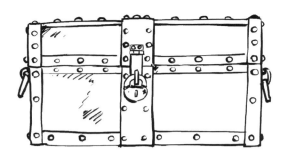

VOCABULARY

Memorize the following vocabulary words, including the genitives and genders for nouns and the four principal parts for verbs.

WORD	DERIVATIVE	TRANSLATION
1. uxor, uxoris, *f.*	_____	*wife*
2. marītus, -ī, *m.*	_____	*husband, bridegroom*
3. arca, -ae, *f.*	_____	*chest, box*
4. operculum, -ī, *n.*	_____	*lid, cover*
5. fundus, -ī, *m.*	_____	*bottom, base*
6. aer, aeris, *m.*	_____	*air*
7. ala, -ae, *f.*	_____	*wing*
8. malum, -i, *n.**	_____	*an evil, a trouble*
9. terreō, -ēre, terruī, territum	_____	*frighten*
10. compleō, -ēre, complēvī, complētum	_____	*fill, fill up*
11. arceō, -ēre, arcuī, ---------	_____	*shut in*
12. caveō, -ēre, cāvī, cautum	_____	*guard against, beware*
13. temptō, -āre, -āvī, -ātum	_____	*try, attempt*
14. evolō, -āre, -āvī, -ātum	_____	*fly out of, fly away from*

* Not to be confused with *mālum* (apple)

15. iaceō, -ēre, iacuī, ------   _____ *lie (flat)*

16. fleō, -ēre, flēvī, flētum   _____ *weep*

17. exspectō, -āre, -āvī, -ātum   _____ *wait for, expect*

18. intra *(prep. with acc.)*   _____ *inside*

19. repente *(adv.)*   _____ *suddenly*

20. nōn *(adv.)*   _____ *not*

REVIEW WORDS

1. avis, avis, *f.*   *bird*
2. bracchium, -ī, *n.*   *arm*
3. cibus, -ī, *m.*   *food*
4. habeō, -ēre, habuī, habitum   *have, hold*
5. mālum*, -ī, *n.*   *apple*
6. narrō, -āre, -āvī, -ātum   *tell*
7. possum, posse, potui, -----   *be able*
8. sedeō, -ēre, sēdī, sessum   *sit*

A. PLUPERFECT & FUTURE PERFECT TENSES (1ST & 2ND CONJUGATIONS)

Like the perfect tense, the pluperfect and future perfect tense endings are added to the *perfect stem* which is formed from the third principal part of the verb. The pluperfect tense refers to an action completed before some time in the past. For example, *I had learned to walk by the time I was two years old.*

Pluperfect (Helping verb — *had*)

fueram — *I had*	fuerāmus — *we had*
fuerās — *you had*	fuerātis — *you (pl.) had*
fuerat — *he, she, it had*	fuerant — *they had*

Now let's add these endings to the perfect stem of portā (*portāv-*):

portāveram — *I had carried*	portāverāmus — *we had carried*
portāverās — *you had carried*	portāverātis — *you (pl.) had carried*
portāverat — *he, she, it had carried*	portāverant- *they had carried*

The future perfect tense refers to an action completed before some point in the future:

> *By this time tomorrow I will have finished my paper.*

Consider the endings and examples below.

Future Perfect (Helping verbs — *will have*)

fuerō — *I will have*	fuerimus — *we will have*
fueris — *you will have*	fueritis — *you (pl.) will have*
fuerit — *he, she, it will have*	fuerint — *they will have*

portāverō — *I will have carried*	portāverimus — *we will have carried*
portāveris — *you will have carried*	portāveritis — *you (pl.) will have carried*
portāverit — *he, she, it will have carried*	portāverint — *they will have carried*

Study the diagram below which shows which tenses are formed from different principal parts of a first or second conjugation verb:

FIRST PART	SECOND PART (Used for present stem)	THIRD PART (Used for perfect stem)	FOURTH PART
	Active and Passive Voice: present tense imperfect tense future tense	Active Voice only: perfect tense pluperfect tense future perfect tense	Passive Voice only: perfect tense pluperfect tense future perfect tense

Fill in the blank petals of the Latin flower below with the *perfect, pluperfect, and future perfect endings* in the active voice. These all attach to the PERFECT STEM.

Perfect Verb Stem

B. PLUPERFECT AND FUTURE PERFECT

Tranlsate verbs from the *pluperfect and future perfect tenses* into English.

1. arcuērant   _____

2. temptāverint   _____

3. iacuerit   _____

4. flēverō   _____

5. evolāverāmus   _____

6. cāveritis   _____

7. complēverās   _____

8. terruerat   _____

9. exspectāveram   _____

10. monuerimus   _____

C. VERB PRACTICE

Translate verbs from all six tenses into English.

1. arcēbat   _____

2. temptāvistī   _____

3. iacet   _____

4. flēbunt   _____

5. evōlāverās   _____

6. cāverint   _____

7. complēbam _____

8. terruerāmus _____

9. exspectābis _____

10. monueris _____

Challenge: iacuērunt _____

D. TRANSLATION: ENGLISH TO LATIN

Translate the following sentences into Latin.

1. The woman had held (her) husband's box. _____

_____

2. The husband will have lifted the lid of the box. _____

_____

3. Julia's brother had shut in Claudius. _____

_____

4. Claudius had lain in the man's box. _____

_____

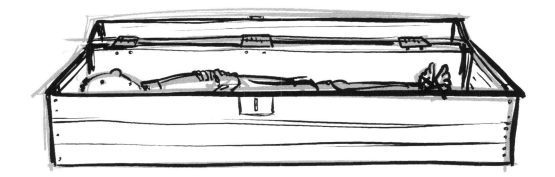

E. REVIEW

Answer the following review questions:

1. How do you find the present stem of a verb?_____

_____

2. Name the helping verbs for the perfect tense. _____

3. Give the four principal parts of the verb *dō*. _____

4. How do you find the perfect stem of a verb?_____

_____

5. Translate these sentences and circle whether they are active or passive:

Saxum in arcā arcēbātur. _____

   Active or Passive?

Saxum Iūlium in arcā arcēbat. _____

_____

   Active or Passive?

10 Lesson Ten

A. DATIVE CASE (1ST, 2ND & 2ND DECLENSTION NEUTER NOUNS)

In Latin, the indirect object is put in the *dative case*. The dative case is used to show *to* or *for* whom something is done, said, given, or shown. It is usually placed in front of the direct object. Consider the following examples:

SN	IO	DO	V-t

Amīcus Iūliae equum dat.

SN V-t IO DO
A friend gives Julia a horse.

SN V-t DO P OP
or *A friend gives a horse to Julia.*

Notice that the word *Iūliae*, which is in the dative case, can be translated in two ways. In the first example it is a true indirect object; in the second the preposition *to* is used. *For* can also be used in some instances. Now let's have a little fun with our example and play "Musical Parts of Speech":

SN IO DO V-t
Iūlia equō amīcum dat.

SN V-t IO DO
Julia gives the horse a friend.

SN V-t DO P OP
or *Julia gives a friend to the horse.*

SN IO DO V-t
Equus amicō Iūliam dat.

SN V-t IO DO
The horse gives a friend Julia.

SN V-t DO P OP
or *The horse gives Julia to a friend.*

By changing the endings we can change the function (part of speech) of a word. Because some endings look the same (1st Declension genitive singular, dative singular, nominative plural and 2nd Declension genitive singular and nominative plural) you need to also use common sense and context clues. Sometimes more than one possibility exists.

B. TRANSLATION: LATIN TO ENGLISH

Translate the following sentences into English. Some contain indirect objects. Some also contain possessive nouns.

1. Iūlia Claudiae et Saxō fābulam dē uxore* et maritō narrābat. _____

_____

2. Uxor maritō arcam dederat. _____

_____

3. Maritus temptāvit operculum levāre. _____

_____

4. Maritus nōn potest operculum levāre. _____

_____

5. Uxor maritō ferramentum dedit et maritum iūvit operculum levāre. _____

_____

_____

* ablative form of *uxor*

68 Lesson Ten

6. Marītus intra arcam spectāvit. _____

_____

7. Repente avis arcam evolāvit et in bracchiō marītī sedit!_____

_____

8. Uxor marītō dōnum dederat! _____

_____

C. TRANSLATION: ENGLISH TO LATIN

Translate the following Pattern 3 sentences into Latin.

1. Claudia had given Julius's horse food _____

_____

2. Saxum will have told the children stories._____

_____

3. The children will have given (their) friends gifts._____

_____

D. PASSIVE VERB PRACTICE:

Translate the following sentences containing passive verbs:

1. Fābulae narrābantur _____

2. Arceor arcam. _____

3. Narrābiminī. _____

4. Exspectābāmur _____

5. Claudius will not be frightened. _____

Challenge: Make up your own sentence using a passive voice verb. Translate your sentence into Latin.

_____

_____

_____

E. REVIEW

Answer the following review questions:

1. What case shows possession? _____

2. How do we show possession in English? _____

3. Which principal part of the verb is used for the *perfect, pluperfect, and future perfect tenses?*

_____

4. How do you find the *present stem* of the verb? _____

_____

11 Lesson Eleven

A. VERB STEM PRACTICE:

Highlight the present and perfect stems for these verbs and identify the conjugation:

Principal Parts

1st	2nd	3rd	4th	Conjugation
1. moneō	monēre	monuī	monitum	_____
2. portō	portāre	portāvī	portātum	_____
3. terreō	terrēre	terruī	territum	_____
4. caveō	cavēre	cāvī	cautum	_____

B. ABLATIVE OF TIME *WHEN* & ABLATIVE OF TIME *DURING*

When you want to talk about something which happens at a specific time, use the *Ablative of Time When*. This ablative is expressed by a noun in the ablative case without a preposition.

Review the ordinal numbers below which can describe the hour of the day. Because the Latin word for hour *-hōrā-* is feminine, the ordinal numbers are also feminine.

prīmā hōrā	*first hour*
secundā hōrā	*second hour*
tertiā hōrā	*third hour*
quartā hōrā	*fourth hour*
quintā hōrā	*fifth hour*
sextā hōrā	*sixth hour*
septimā hōrā	*seventh hour*
octāvā hōrā	*eighth hour*
nōnā hōrā	*ninth hour*
decimā hōrā	*tenth hour*

For example, Julius might agree to help Claudius *at the third hour,* a very precise time.

The *Ablative of Time During* looks just the same but is less precise. Julius might agree to help Claudius *during* the third hour. He will help Claudius *sometime* during the third hour but not right at the third hour. Here is the Latin version:

> *Iūlius Claudium iūvābit tertiā horā.*

The ablative phrase *tertiā horā* can mean "at the third hour" or "during the third hour".

C. TRANSLATION: LATIN TO ENGLISH

Translate the sentences below. Especially watch for the perfect, pluperfect, and future perfect verb tenses and the genitive and dative noun cases, as well as the ablatives of time when and time during.

1. Iūlia fābulam Aesōpī narrāverat tertiā hōrā. _____

_____

2. Frāter Iūliae fābulam nōn auscultāvit. _____

_____

3. Claudius Iūliō et Saxō arcam dēmōnstrāverit quartā hōrā. _____

_____

_____

4. Iūlia īram habuit quod frāter et amīcī nōn auscultāvērunt. _____

_____

_____

5. Iūlius et amīcī Iūliae arcam dederint quintā hōrā._____

_____

_____

D. TRANSLATION: ENGLISH TO LATIN

Translate these passive voice verbs into Latin.

1. It will be shut in. _____

2. We were tried. _____

3. They are lifted. _____

E. TIDBIT

For the Romans, the first hour of the day was approximately 7 a.m.

The sixth hour of the day was around noon.

The twelfth hour was about 6 p.m.

The length of the hours varied with the seasons, becoming shorter during the winter months.

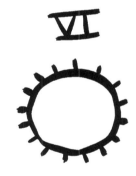

12 Lesson Twelve
The Story of Pandora

Translate the myth *The Story of Pandora*. You do not have to label unless you are having difficulty on a particular sentence. In that case, labeling may help.

1. Epimētheus frāter Promēthēī erat. _____

_____

2. Epimētheus Promētheum iūverat ad virōs ignem apportāre. _____

_____

3. Iuppiter īram habuit contrā Epimētheum et Promētheum. _____

_____

4. Iuppiter Epimētheō poenam creāvit. _____

_____

5. Iuppiter Epimētheō fēminam pulchram formāvit. _____

_____

6. Fēmina Pandōra nominābātur. _____

_____

7. Deī et deae Iovem iūverant fēminam formāre et Pandōrae multa dōna dederant. _____

_____

_____

8. Venus Pandōrae formam dedit et Apollo mūsicam dedit. _____

_____

9. Mercūrius Pandōrae persuāsiōnem dedit. _____

_____

10. Sed Minerva Pandōram cūriōsam formāvit. _____

_____

11. Mercūrius Pandōrae arcam dē Iōve dedit. _____

_____

12. Mercūrius , "Nē levā*," inquit, "operculum arcae." _____

_____

13. Quamquam Prōmētheus Epimētheum monuerat dē dōnō Iōvis Epimētheus Pandōram adhūc amāvit.

_____

_____

14. Pandōra cūriōsa erat. _____

15. Cotidiē Pandōra rogāvit, "Quid est in arcā?" _____

_____

16. Marītus Pandōrae Pandōram monuerat, "Nē temptā** levāre operculum arcae." _____

_____

_____

17. Sed Pandōra marītum nōn auscultāvit. _____

_____

* Imperative of levo
** Imperavative of tempto

Lesson Twelve

18. Operculum arcae levāvit et multa mala arcam evolāvērunt._____

_____

19. Pandōra flēverat quod invīdia, avāritia, morbus, et cūrae arcā evolāvērant. _____

_____

_____

20. Pandōra vōcem parvam auscultāvit et intrā arcam spectāvit._____

_____

21. Spēs iacuit in fundō arcae. _____

_____

22. Pandōra rīsit quod spem habuit. _____

_____

N.B. *Nē* makes a command negative.

MYTH GLOSSARY

1. adhūc (adv.)	*still*
2. Apollo	*god of archery, music, poetry, prophecy*
3. contra (pre. w/acc)	*against*
4. cotidiē	*every day*
5. cūra, -ae, *f.*	*care, worry*
6. cūriōsus, -a, -um	*curious*
7. dea, -ae, *f.*	*goddess*
8. Epimētheus, -ī, *m.*	*brother of Prometheus*
9. erat	*he, she, it was*
10. formō, -āre, -āvī, -ātum	*form, shape, fashion*
11. Iuppiter, Iōvis m.	*Jupiter, king of the gods*
12. Mercūrius, -ī, *m.*	*Mercury, messenger of the gods*
13. Minerva, -ae, *f.*	*goddess of wisdom*
14. multus, -a, -um	*much, many*

15. nominō, -āre, -āvī, -ātum   *name (verb)*
16. parvus, -a, -um   *little*
17. persuāsiō, -ōnis, *f.*   *persuasion*
18. pulcher, pulchra, pulchrum   *beautiful, handsome*
19. quamquam   *although*
20. quid est   *What is, What is it?*
21. rideō, -ēre, rīsī, rīsum   *smile, laugh*
22. rogō, -āre, -āvī, -ātum   *ask*
23. spectō, -āre, -āvī, -ātum   *look at*
24. Venus   *goddess of love and beauty*
25. vox, vōcis, *f.*   *voice*
26. forma, -ae, *f.*   *shape, beauty*

Unit Two Review

A. STEM REVIEW

Give the present and perfect verb stems for the following verbs:

VERB	PRESENT STEM	PERFECT STEM
1. portō		
2. moneō		
3. fleō		
4. terreō		

B. VERB REVIEW

<u>Underline</u> the endings on the verbs below and then translate. All six active verb tenses are represented.

1. apportāvistī _____

2. ēvolat _____

3. temptāverō _____

4. portāverātis _____

5. flēbis _____

6. terrent _____

7. levāverant _____

8. iacēbāmus _____

9. exspectāvimus _____

10. monuerit _____

11. arcuērunt _____

12. cavēbimus _____

C. CONJUGATION

Conjugate and translate the verb *fleo, flere, flevi, fletum* in all six verb tenses.

PRESENT

fleō —	

IMPERFECT

flebām —	

FUTURE

flēbō —	

PERFECT

flēvī —	

PLUPERFECT

flēveram —	

FUTURE PERFECT

flēverō —	

D. CASE REVIEW

Fill in the blanks about the genitive and dative dative cases:

Nominative: subject noun, predicate noun, predicate adjective

Genitive: _____, _____, _____, _____

Dative: _____, _____, _____

Accusative: direct object, object of preposition

Ablative: Place where, Place from which, Time when, Time during

Unit Two Review 81

E. FLOWER REVIEW

Fill in the flower petals with the correct verb tense endings for the present stem and the perfect stem. Draw both active and passive petals for the present stem.

PRESENT STEM (present, imperfect, and future)

Present Verb Stem

PERFECT STEM (perf., pluperf., fut. perf.)

Perfect Verb Stem

F. TRANSLATION: LATIN TO ENGLISH

Translate the sentences below. Especially watch for the perfect, pluperfect, and future perfect tenses and the genitive and dative noun cases. Also look for the ablatives of time when and time during.

1. Iūlius Claudiō benevolentiam dēmonstrāvit sextā horā. _____

_____

2. Uxor marītī intrā arcam spectāverat._____

_____

3. Saxum mūsicam Claudiae auscultāverit tertiā hōrā. _____

_____

4. Fēmina Saxō et Iūliae cibum dedit. _____

_____

5. Monuimus līberōs dē poenā. _____

6. Frāter operculum arcae levāverat sed nōn potuit malum arcēre. _____

_____

G. PASSIVE REVIEW

Translate these passive verbs from the present, imperfect, and future tenses.

1. temptābatur _____

2. complentur _____

3. monēbimur _____

H. DERIVATIVES

Tell the Latin origin for each of the derivatives below. All are from Lists 3 and 4.

DERIVATIVE   **LATIN ORIGIN**

1. temptation   _____

2. fundamental   _____

3. avarice   _____

4. benevolence   _____

Unit 3

5 List Five

VOCABULARY

Memorize the following vocabulary words, including the genitive and gender for nouns and the four principal parts for verbs.

WORD	DERIVATIVE	TRANSLATION
1. fīlius, -ī, *m.*	_____	*son*
2. rēgia, -ae, *f.*	_____	*palace*
3. patria, -ae, *f.*	_____	*native land, country*
4. humus, -ī, *f.*	_____	*ground, earth, land*
5. perīculum, -ī, *n.*	_____	*danger*
6. aurum, -ī, *n.*	_____	*gold*
7. argentum, -ī , *n.*	_____	*silver*
8. mundus,-ī, *m.*	_____	*world*
9. lūna, -ae, *f.*	_____	*moon*
10. stella, -ae, *f.*	_____	*star*
11. astrum -ī , *n.*	_____	*constellation*
12. stō, -āre, stetī, statum	_____	*stand*
13. rogō, -āre, -āvī, -ātum	_____	*ask*
14. properō, -āre, -āvī, -ātum	_____	*hasten, hurry*

15. lūceō, -ēre, lūxī, ----- _____ *shine*

16. perīculōsus, -a, -um _____ *dangerous*

17. aureus, -a, -um _____ *golden*

18. argenteus, -a, -um _____ *silver, silvery*

19. altus, -a, -um _____ *high, deep*

20. lūcidus, -a, -um _____ *bright*

REVIEW WORDS

1. Aesōpus, -ī, *m.*   *Aesop*
2. agītō, -āre, -āvī, -ātum   *drive*
3. ambulō, -āre, -āvī, -ātum   *walk*
4. amīcus, -ī, *m.*   *friend*
5. compleō, -ēre,-ēvī, ētum   *fill, fill up*
6. deus, -ī, *m.*   *god*
7. domus, -ūs, *f.*   *house, home*
8. equus, -ī, *m.*   *horse*
9. fabricō, -āre, -āvī, -ātum   *make, forge*
10. fīlia, -ae, *f.*   *daughter*
11. moneō, -ēre, -uī, -itum   *warn*
12. narrātor, narratōris, *m.*   *storyteller*
13. narrō, -āre, -āvī, -ātum,   *tell, relate, recount*
14. prope (*prep w/acc.*)   *near*
15. pugnō, -āre, -āvī, -ātum   *fight*
16. rēgīna, -ae, *f.*   *queen*
17. rēx, rēgis, *m.*   *king*
18. rīdeō, -ēre, rīsī, rīsum   *laugh, smile*
19. sōl, sōlis, *m.*   *sun*
20. terreō, -ēre, -uī, -itum   *frighten*
21. vēritās, vēritātis, *f.*   *truth*

(13) Lesson Thirteen

A. VERB SYNOPSES

We have learned all six verb tenses in the active voice, as well as three tenses (the present, imperfect, and future) in the passive voice. Now we will learn how to do a *verb synopsis*. A verb synopsis is a summary of a verb in a particular person and number in all six verb tenses. It can be a summary in both the active and passive voices. Below is an example of a verb synopsis for *amō* in first person singular, active and passive voices:

AMO, AMARE, AMAVI, AMATUM — FIRST PERSON SINGULAR

Tense	Synopsis (Active Voice)	Translation
Present	amō	*I love, am loving, do love*
Imperfect	amābam	*I was loving, used to love*
Future	amābō	*I will love*
Perfect	amāvī	*I loved, have loved, did love*
Pluperfect	amāveram	*I had loved*
Future Perfect	amāverō	*I will have loved*

Tense	Synopsis (Passive Voice)	Translation
Present	amor	*I am (being) loved*
Imperfect	amābar	*I was (being) loved*
Future	amābor	*I will be loved*

Now do verb synopses for the following verbs according to the person, number, and voice given.

MONEO, MONERE, MONUI, MONITUM — SECOND PERSON SINGULAR

Tense	Synopsis (Active Voice)	Translation
Present		
Imperfect		
Future		
Perfect		
Pluperfect		
Future Perfect		

Tense	Synopsis (Passive Voice)	Translation
Present		
Imperfect		
Future		

TERREO, TERRERE, TERRUI, TERRITUM — THIRD PERSON SINGULAR

Tense	Synopsis (Active)	Translation
Present		
Imperfect		
Future		
Perfect		
Pluperfect		
Future Perfect		

Tense	Synopsis (Active)	Translation
Present		
Imperfect		
Future		

92 Lesson Thirteen

NARRO, NARRARE, NARRAVI, NARRATUM — **FIRST PERSON PLURAL**

Tense	Synopsis (Active Voice)	Translation
Present		
Imperfect		
Future		
Perfect		
Pluperfect		
Future Perfect		

Tense	Synopsis (Passive Voice)	Translation
Present		
Imperfect		
Future		

AGITO, AGITARE, AGITAVI, AGITATUM — **SECOND PERSON PLURAL**

Tense	Synopsis (Active Voice)	Translation
Present		
Imperfect		
Future		
Perfect		
Pluperfect		
Future Perfect		

Tense	Synopsis (Passive Voice)	Translation
Present		
Imperfect		
Future		

FABRICO, FABRICARE, FABRICAVI, FABRICATUM — **THIRD PERSON PLURAL**

Tense	Synopsis (Active Voice)	Translation
Present		
Imperfect		
Future		
Perfect		
Pluperfect		
Future Perfect		

Tense	Synopsis (Passive Voice)	Translation
Present		
Imperfect		
Future		

B. BUILDING BLOCKS

Translate the "building block" sentences below.

1. Iūlia narrat. _____

2. Iūlia fābulam narrābat._____

3. Iūlia Claudiō et Claudiae fābulam narrābit. _____

_____

4. Iūlia Claudiō et Claudiae fābulam Aesōpī narrāvit. _____

_____

5. Iūlia et Iūlius līberīs fābulās Aesōpī nōn narrāverant. _____

_____

6. Iūlia et Iūlius amīcīs fābulās līberōrum narrāverint. _____

_____

C. REVIEW — ANSWER THE FOLLOWING QUESTIONS:

1. What is the present stem of *properō*? _____

2. What is the perfect stem of *stō?*_____

3. What case do direct objects go in? _____

4. What case do indirect objects go in?_____

5. Which principal part of the verb is used to form the stem for the *present, imperfect,* and *future tenses, passive voice?* _____

6. What are the helping verbs for the perfect tense, active voice? _____

D. DERIVATIVE DIGGING

Choose ten derivatives from List Five and use them correctly in a short paragraph or story. Underline the derivatives.

_____

_____

_____

_____

_____

_____

_____

_____

_____

_____

14 Lesson Fourteen

A. SUM (THE LINKING VERB) AND PREDICATE NOUNS

The "linking verb" (or being verb as it is sometimes called) is unique in many languages. Latin and English are no exceptions. In both languages the spelling of this verb is irregular. The four principal parts are also irregular: *sum, esse, fuī, futurum*. Unlike other verbs which *do* something or show *action*, the linking verb is simply the verb of existence. The subject of a linking verb does not *do* anything. The infinitive of the linking verb, *esse*, means "to be." The linking verb is conjugated in all six tenses below. When "being" appears in parentheses, it is optional.

PRESENT TENSE

sum — *I am (being)*	sumus — *we are (being)*
es — *you are (being)*	estis — *you (pl.) are (being)*
est — *he, she, it is (being)*	sunt — *they are (being)*

IMPERFECT TENSE

eram — *I was (being)*	erāmus — *we were (being)*
erās — *you were (being)*	erātis — *you (pl.) were (being)*
erat — *he, she, it was (being)*	erant — *they were (being)*

FUTURE TENSE

erō — *I will be*	erimus — *we will be*
eris — *you will be*	eritis — *you (pl.) will be*
erit — *he, she, it will be*	erunt — *they will be*

PERFECT TENSE

fuī — *I have been*	fuimus — *we have been*
fuistī — *you have been*	fuistis — *you (pl.) have been*
fuit — *he, she, it has been*	fuērunt — *they have been*

PLUPERFECT TENSE

fueram — *I had been*	fuerāmus — *we had been*
fuerās — *you had been*	fuerātis — *you (pl.) had been*
fuerat — *he, she, it had been*	fuerant — *they had been*

FUTURE PERFECT TENSE

fuerō — *I will have been*	fuerimus — *we will have been*
fueris — *you will have been*	fueritis — *you (pl.) will have been*
fuerit — *he, she, it will have been*	fuerint — *they will have been*

As you memorize the different tenses of the linking verb, be careful not to confuse its imperfect and future tenses with the *active voice endings* of the pluperfect and future perfect tenses. Remember, those are *endings* which coincidentally look like the imperfect and future of *sum*. They cannot stand alone but must be attached to some verb stem and are translated as the helping verbs *had* (pluperfect) or *will have* (future perfect). The linking verbs always stand alone and do not help any other verbs. Study the examples below and see how the meaning changes between the sentences containing an active verb and a linking verb.

    SN   V-t   DO
    Iūlia narrāv**erat** fābulam.   *Julia **had** told a story.*

    SN LV PrN
    Iūlia **erat** fābula.   *Julia **was** a story.*

When comparing Pattern 2 sentences (SN- V-t — DO) with Pattern 4 sentences (SN — LV-PrN), it is helpful to ask this question regarding direct objects and predicate nouns:

Does *fābulam* mean the same thing as *Iūlia*? If the answer is no then *fābulam* is a direct object. If the answer is yes then *fābula* is a predicate noun.

> SN   V-t   DO
> Iūlius terru**erit** equum.   *Julius **will have** frightened the horse.*

> SN   LV   PrN
> Iūlius **erit** equus.   *Julius **will be** a horse.*

The linking verb is also distinct because it does not take a direct object in its predicate. Instead, it is followed by a *predicate noun* . In Latin, the predicate noun is sometimes called the predicate nominative. This is because a noun which follows the linking verb is put in the nominative case. Compare the following examples:

> SN   V-t   DO
> Fēmina spectat lūnam.   *The woman looks at the moon.*

> SN   LV PrN
> Fēmina est lūna.   *The woman is a moon.*

Note that in the first example, the direct object *moon* is not the same thing as the subject noun *woman*. In the second example the subject noun and predicate noun are the same—the woman is also the moon. In sentences containing linking verbs, the linking verb is like the equal sign in an equation:

> 2 + 2   =   4
> SN   LV   PrN

2 + 2 is another way of saying 4. The predicate noun is another way of saying the subject noun.

It is also possible to have a predicate noun without a subject noun. In that case, the subject is derived from the verb ending:

> LV   PrN
> Est fēmina.   *She is a woman.*

Nota bene: Frequently, the linking verb is last in the sentence and the predicate noun may precede it. For example, *Fēmina lūna est* is translated as *The woman is a moon.*

B. TRANSLATION: LATIN TO ENGLISH

Translate the following sentences containing linking verbs into English. Many will also contain predicate nouns.

1. Amīcī fuerāmus. _____

2. Sōl est stella. _____

3. Fuistis discipulī. _____

4. Puerī virī erunt. _____

5. Nārrātor Aesōpus erat. _____

6. Fuerō magister/magistra. _____

C. TRANSLATION: ENGLISH TO LATIN

Translate the following sentences into Latin:

1. I am a girl/boy (choose one). _____

2. You have been a teacher. _____

3. The box was a gift. _____

4. The flames will be a fire. _____

5. The man's iron tool will have been a weapon. _____

_____

6. You had been a storyteller. _____

D. SYNOPSIS

Do a synopsis of *sum* in the first person plural. Note that *sum* is neither active or passive but is in a class by itself.

Tense	Synopsis	Translation
present		
imperfect		
future		
perfect		
pluperfect		
future perfect		

Don't confuse passive voice verbs with the linking verb. Consider the examples below:

SN   LV   PrN
Pandōra est fēmina.   *Pandora is a woman.*

SN   V (passive)
Pandōra monētur.   *Pandora is warned.*

The linking verb is followed by a predicate noun in the first example. In the second example, the subject is followed by a passive verb.

E. ETYMOLOGY

Choose a derivative from List 5 and write its *etymology* on the lines below.

Derivative: _____

Etymology: _____

_____

6 List Six

VOCABULARY

Memorize the following vocabulary words, including the genitive and gender for nouns, and the four principal parts for verbs.

WORD	DERIVATIVE	TRANSLATION
1. Apollō, Apollinis, *m.*		*sun god*
2. Vulcānus, -ī, *m.*		*god of fire*
3. Phaethōn, Phaethōnis, *m.*		*son of Apollo*
4. diēs, diēī, *m.*		*day*
5. mensis, mensis, *m.*		*month*
6. annus, -ī, *m.*		*year*
7. vēr, vēris, *n.*		*spring*
8. aestās, aestātis, *f.*		*summer*
9. autumnus, -ī, *m.*		*autumn*
10. hiems, hiemis, *f.*		*winter*
11. taurus, -ī, *m.*		*bull*
12. scorpiō, scorpiōnis, *m.*		*scorpion*
13. sagittārius, -ī, *m.*		*archer*
14. habēna, -ae, *f.*		*strap, rein*
15. fulmen, fulminis, *n.*		*thunderbolt, lightning*

16. optātum, -ī, *n.* _____ *a wish*

17. ornō, -āre, -āvī, -ātum _____ *equip, decorate*

18. iactō, -āre, -āvī, -ātum _____ *throw*

19. implōrō, -āre, -āvī, -ātum _____ *beg, implore*

20. optō, -āre, -āvī, -ātum _____ *wish for, desire, want*

REVIEW WORDS

This review list consists of adjectives we have encountered in this book and in previous books. You will need to refer to it when doing the exercises in the lessons to come.

1. albus, -a, -um — *white*
2. argenteus, -a, -um — *silvery*
3. aureus, -a, -um — *golden*
4. bonus, -a, -um* — *good*
5. citus, -a, -um** — *fast, swift*
6. dēfessus, -a, -um — *tired*
7. longus, -a -um — *long*
8. magnus, -a, -um — *large, great*
9. multus, -a, -um — *much, many*
10. parvus, -a, -um — *small*
11. pulcher, pulchra, pulchrum — *beautiful, handsome*
12. stultus, -a, -um — *foolish*
13. superbus, -a,-um — *proud*
14. tardus, -a, -um — *slow*

* The adverb of this word is *bene*, which means *well*.

** The adverb of this word is *cito*.

In Lesson Eleven we already touched on ordinal numbers, which are also adjectives. There we used the ordinal numbers to express the ablative of time when.

1. prīmus, -a, -um   *first*
2. secundus, -a, -um   *second*
3. tertius, -a, -um   *third*
4. quartus, -a, -um   *fourth*
5. quīntus, -a, -um   *fifth*
6. sextus, -a,-um   *sixth*
7. septimus, -a, -um   *seventh*
8. octāvus, -a, -um   *eighth*
9. nōnus, -a, -um   *ninth*
10. decimus, -a, -um   *tenth*

15 Lesson Fifteen

A. ADJECTIVES & PREDICATE ADJECTIVES

An adjective modifies a noun or a pronoun. It can tell which one, what kind, and how many. Unlike English, Latin adjectives frequently follow the nouns they describe. Consider these examples:

> Fīlius stultus taurōs dēfessōs agitābat.
> *The foolish son was driving the tired bulls.*

> Fīlius stultus taurōs dēfessōs amīcī bonī agitābat.
> *The foolish son was driving (his) good friend's tired bulls.*

The adjectives *stultus, bonī,* and *dēfessūs* come after the nouns they describe, but notice that they also match those nouns in *gender, number,* and *case.* Each adjective has three endings which correspond to the three genders: *-us* is masculine, *-a* is feminine, and *-um* is neuter. Notice also that the adjectives match the nouns in *number.* If a noun is singular, the adjective which modifies it is singular, and if it is plural, the adjective which modifies it is also plural. Finally, if a noun is in a particular case, the adjective which describes it must also be in that case. In the example above, the adjective *stultus* is in the nominative singular case because *fīlius* in the nominative singular case. *Bonī* is in the genitive singular case because it modifies the noun *amicī* is in the genitive singular case. *Dēfessōs* is in the accusative plural case because it modifies the noun *taurōs* which is in the accusative plural case.

Consider these feminine examples:

Lūna argenta lūcet.	*The silvery moon shines.*
Lūnam argentam spectant.	*They look at the silvery moon.*

Now examine some neuter examples:

Dēmōnstrābat oppidum prīmum.	*He was showing the first town.*
Dēmōnstrābat fīliō bonō oppidum prīmum.	*He was showing (his) good son the first town.*

Predicate Adjectives

A predicate adjective is different from regular adjectives because it must accompany the linking verb.

It will always modify the subject noun and, like a predicate noun, must agree with the noun it describes in gender, number, and case (which will, of course, be nominative). Look over the examples below:

Puella est bona.	*The girl is good.*
Puellae sunt bonae.	*The girls are good.*
Amīcus est bonus.	*The friend is good.*
Amīcī sunt bonī.	*The friends are good.*
Dōnum est bonum.	*The gift is good.*
Dōna sunt bona.	*The gifts are good.*

Fill in the blanks below about adjectives.

1. Adjectives must match the nouns they describe in *gender, number, and case.*

2. What are the three genders?

_____, _____, _____

3. What gender uses the *-us* ending?   _____

   What gender uses the *-a* ending?   _____

   What gender uses the *-um* ending?   _____

4. What is meant by *number?*_____ or _____

5. What are the five noun cases?

   _____

   _____

   _____

   _____

   _____

B. TRANSLATION: LATIN TO ENGLISH

Translate these sentences containing adjectives.

1. Līberī et Saxum caelum magnum spectābant._____

_____

2. Lūna alba et stellae argenteae in caelō magnō lūcēbant. _____

_____

3. Saxum stellās multās et astra multa dēmōnstrābat. _____

_____

4. Iūlia Scorpium superbum videt. _____

5. "Taurus," Iūlius inquit*, "est magnus." _____

6. Claudia et Claudius Saxō Scorpium perīculōsum dēmōnstrāvērunt. _____

_____

7. "Sōl," Saxum inquit, "est stella aurea mundī nostrī.** _____

_____

*_Inquit_ means "he, she, it said." _Inquit_ is used when a direct quotation is used. In English, we would use quotation marks.
**_Nostrī_ is from the adjective _noster, nostra, nostrum_ which means "our".

C. VERB SYNOPSIS REVIEW

Fill in the verb synopsis below according to the formula given.

Translate the verb *ornō, ornāre, ornāvī, ornātum* in the third person singular, active voice.

Tense	Synopsis	Translation
present		
imperfect		
future		
perfect		
pluperfect		
future perfect		

Now translate the same verb in the third person singular, passive voice.

Tense	Synopsis	Translation
Present		
Imperfect		
Future		

D. TIDBIT

The Romans used sundials to mark the time of day. The sundial enabled them to divide the day into twelve sections or hours. The first hour of the day was about seven A.M. The Romans also used water clocks in which water passed through at a certain rate. It took two water clocks to equal one hour. Water clocks were sometimes used to time speeches in the Roman senate. If the water ran out the speech was over!

16 Lesson Sixteen

A. MORE ABOUT ADJECTIVES

In the last lesson we learned that adjectives must match nouns in gender, number, and case. However, adjectives do not always match the nouns they modify in declension. Consider the first declension nouns below. Although they are from first declension, they are not feminine, but masculine.

> **P**oēta (*poet*) and **P**īrāta (*pirate*)
> **A**gricola (*farmer*)
> **I**ncola (*settler*)–can be masculine or feminine
> **N**auta (*sailor*)

This group of nouns is sometimes known as the "pain" words because they are masculine exceptions in the usually feminine first declension. In addition, the noun *humus* (ground, earth) is a feminine exception within the masculine second declension. In the sentence below, the adjectives match the nouns they follow in gender, number and case, but they do not match in declension.

> Agricola bon**us** humum bon**am** arāvit.   *The good farmer plowed the good ground.*

Notice that although *agricola* is a first declension noun, it is masculine in gender and requires a masculine adjective. *Humum* (the accusative form of *humus,* a second declension noun) is feminine in gender and requires a feminine adjective. So, an adjective matches the noun it modifies in gender, number, and case but NOT NECESSARILY IN DECLENSION.

Translate these noun-adjective phrases into Latin. Remember to make them agree in gender, number, and case. Use the nominative case.

1. the good poet   *poēta bonus* _____

2. the weary farmer   _____

3. the small sailors   _____

4. the foolish (female) settlers _____

5. the foolish (male) settlers   _____

B. ADVERBS

Adverbs describe a verb, adjective or another adverb. They tell **how, when** and **where**. A Latin adverb is formed by taking the ending off of the **feminine** form of the adjective and adding -ē.

Lūna lūcet pulchrē.	*The moon shines beautifully.*
Fīlius stultus rogābat stultē.	*The foolish son was asking foolishly.*

N.B. The adverb formed from *bonus* is irregular. *Bene* is the adverb form of *bonus* and means *well*.

Form adverbs from the adjectives below and then translate the **adverbs**. One is done as an example.

ADJECTIVE	FEMININE FORM	ADVERB	TRANSLATION
1. tardus, -a, -um	tarda-	tardē	slowly
2. stultus, -a, -um			
3. superbus, -a, -um			
4. dēfessūs, -a, -um			
5. pulcher, pulchra, pulchrum			

C. TRANSLATION: ENGLISH TO LATIN

1. Julia loves the golden autumn. _____

2. She walks swiftly toward Saxum and Claudia. _____

_____

3. The silvery moon shines beautifully. _____

4. A good farmer gives the tired children apples. _____

_____

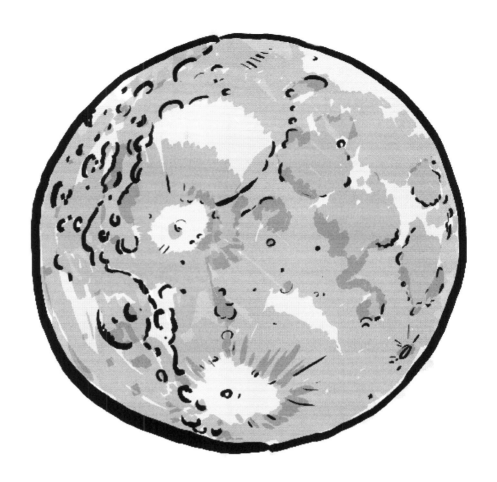

D. TRANSLATION: LATIN TO ENGLISH

Translate the sentences below. Some contain linking verbs.

1. Iūlius nōn erat taurus. _____

2. Iūlius taurum nōn vīderat. _____

3. Scorpius perīculōsus erit. _____

4. Scorpius perīculōsus iacuerit in terrā. _____

_____

5. Erunt amīcī. _____

6. Rogāvērunt amīcōs. _____

(17) Lesson Seventeen

A. ABLATIVE OF MEANS

When an inanimate object or tool is used to accomplish something it is put in the ablative case **without** a Latin preposition. This ablative is often translated using the English preposition *with* or the prepositional phrase *by means of.* Look at the example below:

> Iūlius equum habēnīs habet.
> > *Julius holds the horse with (by means of) the reins.*

> Agricola incolam ferramentō iuverat arāre.
> > *The farmer had helped the settler to plow with (by means of) an iron tool.*

Now translate the sentences below which contain the ablative of means.

1. Puellae et Saxum rēgiam aurō et argentō ornābant. _____

_____

2. Claudius arcam ferramentō fabricāvit. _____

_____

3. Vir perīculum tēlō pugnat. _____

_____

B. VERB SYNOPSIS REVIEW

Fill in the synopses below according to the formulas given:

iactō, -āre, -āvī, -ātum in the third person plural, active voice

Tense	Synopsis	Translation
present		
imperfect		
future		
perfect		
pluperfect		
future perfect		

iactō, -āre,-āvī, -ātum in the third person plural, passive voice

Tense	Synopsis	Translation
present		
imperfect		
future		

sum, esse, fuī, futūrum in the third person plural

Tense	Synopsis	Translation
present		
imperfect		
future		
perfect		
pluperfect		
future perfect		

C. TRANSLATION: LATIN TO ENGLISH

1. Rēx currum ad rēgiam pulchram cito agitat. _____

_____

2. Līberī dēfessī ad domum tarde ambulāvērunt. _____

_____

3. Taurī superbī bene pugnābant. _____

_____

N.B. *Cito* is an irregular adverb.

18 Lesson Eighteen

Phaethon and the Sun God's Chariot

Translate the story of Phaethon.

1. Apollō Deus Sōlis erat. _____

2. Phaethōn fīlius Apollinis erat sed amīcī Phaethōnis eum derīsērunt. _____

_____

3. "Tū," inquiunt, "nōn es fīlius deī." _____

_____

4. Rēgia Apollinis erat in Indiā et Phaethōn properāvit et patrem vīsit._____

_____

5. Rēgia aurea erat pulchra et portās argenteās habēbat. _____

_____

6. Carbunculī, smaragdī, adamantēs, et aliae gemmae rēgiam exornābant._____

_____

7. Diēs, Mensēs, Annī et Hōrae prope Apolline stetērunt._____

_____

8. Vēr, Aestās, Autumna, et Hiems erant in rēgiā Apollinis. _____

_____

9. Phaethōn Apollinem appropinquāvit et Apollō, "Es," inquit, "fīlius meus."_____

_____

10. Apollō Phaethōnem narrāvit et beneficium rogāvit._____

_____

11. Phaethōn optāvit currum Apollinis agitāre._____

_____

12. Apollō Phaethōnem implōrāvit, "Nē agitā currum sōlis, filī mī. Est perīculōsum."

_____

_____

13. Apollō filium monuit sed Phaethōn instābat. _____

_____

14. Apollō Phaethonī* currum aureum dēmōnstrāvit. _____

_____

15. Vulcānus currum fabricāverat et currum gemmīs exornāvit. _____

_____

* *Phaethonī* is dative

16. Lūna et stellae nōn iam lucēbant. _____

_____

17. Apollō et Phaethōn ad currum ambulāvērunt. _____

_____

18. Phaethōn habēnās habuit et equī trāns caelum superbē properāvērunt. _____

_____

19. Phaethōn astra magna timuit; Scorpium, Sagittārium, et Aquārium vidit. _____

_____

_____

20. Currus sōlis Ursum Magnum et Ursum Parvum torruit. _____

_____

21. Patriae, silvae, et agrī ardēbant. _____

_____

22. Phaethōn mundum in flammīs vidit. _____

_____

23. Postrēmō, Iuppiter fulmen iactāvit et Phaethōnem necāvit. _____

_____

GLOSSARY

1. adamās, adamantis, *m.*	*diamond*
2. ager, -agrī, *m.*	*field*
3. alius, -a, -um	*other*
4. appropinquō, -āre, -āvī, -ātum	*approach*
5. aquārius, -ī, *m.*	*water carrier*
6. ardeō, -ēre, arsī, arsum	*burn*

7. beneficium, -ī, *n.*	*favor*	
8. carbunculus, -ī, *m.*	*ruby*	
9. dērīdeō, -ēre, -rīsī, -rīsum	*laugh at, mock*	
10. deus, -ī, *m.*	*god*	
11. eum	*him (acc. sing.)*	
12. exornō, -āre, -āvī, -ātum	*adorn, decorate*	
13. gemma, -ae, *f.*	*jewel*	
14. India, -ae, *f.*	*India*	
15. inquiunt	*they said*	
16. instō, -āre, -stitī, -------	*insist*	
17. meus, -a, -um	*my*	
18. narrō, -āre, -āvī, -ātum	*tell*	
19. necō, -āre, -āvī, -ātum	*kill*	
20. nōn iam	*no longer*	
21. porta, -ae, *f.*	*door, gate*	
22. postrēmō	*finally*	
23. prope *(prep. with abl.)*	*near*	
24. properō, -āre, -āvī, -ātum	*hurry, hasten*	
25. silva, -ae, *f.*	*forest*	
26. smaragdus, -ī, *m.*	*emerald*	
27. sōl, sōlis, *m.*	*sun*	
28. timeō, -ēre, timuī, ------	*fear*	
29. torreō, -ēre, -uī, tostum	*scorch*	
30. trāns	*across*	
31. tū	*you (sing.)*	

A. SYNOPSIS REVIEW

Do the verb synopses below according to the formulas given. Be sure to find the present and perfect verb stems first.

ORNO, -ARE, AVI, ATUM IN SECOND PERSON SINGULAR, ACTIVE VOICE

Tense	Synopsis	Translation
present		
imperfect		
future		
perfect		
pluperfect		
future perfect		

ORNO, IN SECOND PERSON SINGULAR, PASSIVE VOICE

Tense	Synopsis	Translation
present		
imperfect		
future		

B. LINKING VERB SYNOPSIS

Do a synopsis of the linking verb *sum, esse, fuī, futurum* in the third person singular.

Tense	Synopsis	Translation
present		
imperfect		
future		
perfect		
pluperfect		
future perfect		

C. TRANSLATION: LATIN TO ENGLISH

Now translate these sets of sentences. Each set contains a sentence with an active voice verb, a sentence containing a passive voice verb, and a sentence containing a linking verb. Not all the sentences will make sense!

1. Amīcus monēbat. _____

2. Amīcus monēbātur. _____

3. Amīcus erat Iūlius. _____

4. Taurī equōs terrēbunt. _____

_____

5. Taurī terrēbuntur *ab equīs (by the horses).* _____

_____

6. Taurī erunt equī. _____

7. Ornāmus rēgiam. _____

8. Ornāmur prope rēgiam. _____

9. Sumus rēgia. _____

D. ADJECTIVE REVIEW

Translate these sentences containing adjectives or predicate adjectives into Latin. Remember to make each adjective match the noun it describes in *gender, number,* and *case.*

1. Claudius does not tell the long story. _____

_____

2. We were tired. _____

3. You will wish for a golden palace. _____

4. The silvery moon had shone. _____

5. Apollo gave his foolish son the reins of the great horses. _____

_____

6. Julia is first. _____

7. Saxum was second. _____

8. The boys will be proud. _____

E. "PAIN" NOUNS REVIEW

Circle the correct form of the adjectives to match the "PAIN" nouns below. All are in the nominative case.

1. the fourth poet:	poeta	*quarta*	*quartus*	*quartum*
2. the tired farmers:	agricolae	*dēfessī*	*dēfessa*	*dēfessae*
3. the handsome sailor:	nauta	*pulcher*	*pulchra*	*pulchrum*
4. the many settlers:	incolae	*multa*	*multae*	*multi*

Unit Three Review

F. ABLATIVE OF MEANS REVIEW

Fill in the blanks about the *ablative of means* and then translate the sentences:

When an _____ or _____ is used to accomplish something it is put in the ablative case (with/without) a preposition. [circle correct answer]

1. Iuppiter filium Apollinis necāvit fulmine*. _____

_____

2. Vulcānus currum sōlis fabricāvit ferramentō. _____

_____

* *Fulmine* is the ablative form of *fulmen*.

G. DERIVATIVES REVIEW

Choose five derivatives from List 5 and five derivatives from List 6, then write their Latin origins.

DERIVATIVE	LATIN ORIGIN
1. _____	_____
2. _____	_____
3. _____	_____
4. _____	_____
5. _____	_____
6. _____	_____
7. _____	_____
8. _____	_____
9. _____	_____
10. _____	_____

OR...

Correctly use ten derivatives from Lists 5 and 6 in a short paragraph.

_____

_____

_____

_____

_____

_____

_____

_____

Unit 4

7 List Seven

VOCABULARY

Memorize the following vocabulary words, including the genitive and gender for nouns, and the four principal parts for verbs.

WORD	DERIVATIVE	TRANSLATION
1. cēna, -ae, *f.*	_____	*dinner, meal*
2. cibus, -ī, *m.*	_____	*food*
3. folīum, -ī, *n.*	_____	*leaf*
4. rōsa, -ae, *f.*	_____	*rose*
5. vīnum, -ī, *n.*	_____	*wine*
6. rāmus, -ī, *m.*	_____	*branch*
7. rāmulus, -ī, *m.*	_____	*twig*
8. glēba, -ae, *f.*	_____	*dirt clod*
9. mensa, -ae, *f.*	_____	*table*
10. carpō, -ere, carpsī, carptum	_____	*pluck*
11. pōtō, -āre, -āvī, -ātum	_____	*drink*
12. edō, -ere, ēdī, ēsum	_____	*eat*
13. regō, -ere, rēxī, rēctum	_____	*rule, govern*
14. surgō, -ere, surrēxī, surrēctum	_____	*rise, get up*

15. cognōscō, -ere, cognōvī, cognitum _____ *recognize*

16. tangō, -ere, tetīgī, tactum _____ *touch*

17. dūcō, -ere, dūxī, ductum _____ *lead*

18. dīcō, -ere, dīxī, dictum _____ *say, speak, tell*

19. nunc (adv.) _____ *now*

20. inter *(prep. with acc.)* _____ *between, among*

REVIEW WORDS

1. apportō, -āre, -āvī, -ātum   *bring*
2. arbor, arboris, *f.*   *tree*
3. aureus, -a, -um   *golden*
4. aurum, -ī, *n.*   *gold*
5. errō, -āre, -āvī, -ātum   *wander, be mistaken*
6. iactō, -āre, -āvī, -ātum   *throw*
7. lūceō, -ēre, lūxī, -----   *shine*
8. magister, -trī, *m.*   *master, teacher*
9. mālum, -ī, *n.*   *apple*
10. optātum, -ī, *n.*   *a wish*
11. ornō, -āre, -āvī, -ātum   *decorate*
12. parō, -āre, -āvī, -ātum   *prepare*
13. pomārium, -ī, *n.*   *orchard*
14. properō, -āre, -āvī, -ātum   *hurry, hasten*
15. rideō, -ēre, rīsī, rīsum   *laugh, smile*
16. rogō, -āre, -āvī, -ātum   *ask*
17. sedeō, -ēre, sēdī, sessum   *sit*
18. tum (adv.)   *then*

(19) Lesson Nineteen

A. THIRD CONJUGATION VERBS (PRESENT, IMPERFECT & FUTURE TENSES)

Third conjugation verbs are conjugated differently from first and second conjugation verbs in the present, imperfect, and future tenses. We must also learn to recognize third conjugation verbs by comparing the first two principal parts with those of first and second conjugations. *Dūcō (lead)* will be our example for third conjugation:

1st Conjugation	amō, amāre
2nd Conjugation	videō, vidēre
3rd Conjugation	dūcō, dūcere

First conjugation verbs are easily recognized by the *-ā* at the end of the verb stem (which is found by removing the *-re* from *amāre*). Second conjugation verbs have an *-e* before the *ō* in the first principal part and the verb stem ends in *-ē*. To recognize a third conjugation verb, it is necessary to look at both the first and second principal parts. Notice that *dūcō* ends in *-ō* just as *amō* does. But the second principal part, *dūcere*, ends in *-ere*, differing from the *-āre* ending of first conjugation verbs. *Dūcō* also differs from *videō* because it has no *-e* before the *-ō* . In the second principal part, *vidēre* contains a macron over the *-ē* but there is no macron in *dūcere*.

To find the present stem of a third conjugation verb, remove the *-ō* from the first principal part. For instance, the stem of *dūcō* is *dūc-* . Now study *dūcō* as it is conjugated in the present, imperfect, and future tenses and highlight the present stem.

PRESENT TENSE

dūc**ō** — *I lead, am leading, do lead*	dūc**imus** — *we lead, are leading, do lead*
dūc**is** — *you lead, are leading, do lead*	dūc**itis** — *you (pl.) lead, are leading, do lead*
dūc**it** — *he, she, it leads, is leading, does lead*	dūc**unt** — *they lead, are leading, do lead*

N.B. — Instead of the familiar *ō, s, t, mus, tis, nt* endings, third conjugation uses *ō, is, it, imus, itis, unt.*

IMPERFECT TENSE

dūcēbam — *I was leading, used to lead*	dūcēbāmus — *we were leading, used to lead*
dūcēbās — *you were leading, used to lead*	dūcēbātis — *you (pl.) were leading, used to lead*
dūcēbat — *he, she, it was leading, used to lead*	dūcēbant — *they were leading, used to lead*

N.B. — Note the *-ē* in front of the imperfect endings for third conjugation.

FUTURE TENSE

dūcam — *I will lead*	dūcēmus — *we will lead*
dūcēs — *you will lead*	dūcētis — *you (pl.) will lead*
dūcet — *he, she, it will lead*	dūcent — *they will lead*

N.B. This tense differs most from first and second conjugations. Instead of *bō, bis, bit, bimus, bitis, bunt* the future chant for third conjugation is *am, ēs, et, ēmus, ētis, ent.*

B. VERB TRANSLATION

Translate the sets of verbs below into Latin. Each set contains a first, second, and third conjugation verb. The first is done as an example. Use spaces to show groups of 3 verbs.

1. You love.   *Amās*

   You see.   *Vidēs*

   You lead.   *Dūcis*

2. She was drinking. _____

   She was laughing. _____

   She was eating. _____

3. We will decorate. _____

   We will shine. _____

   We will speak. _____

4. You (plural) are throwing. _____

   You (plural) do have. _____

   You (plural) rise. _____

5. They will ask. _____

   They will sit. _____

   They will touch. _____

C. TRANSLATION

Translate the sentences below. Some contain third conjugation verbs.

1. Līberī et Saxum māla carpēbant in pomāriō. _____

_____

2. Rāmī multa māla inter fōlia habuērunt. _____

_____

3. Tum puellae rōsās pulchrās carpēbant sed puerī et Saxum glēbās iactābant. _____

_____

_____

4. Iūlia et Claudia cibum parābant. _____

5. Līberī et Saxum ad mensam sedēbant et cēnam edēbant. _____

_____

6. Nunc Iūlius līberōs et Saxum ad pomārium dūcit et dicit, "Carpite māla!"* _____

_____

*   *Carpite* is a plural command from the verb *carpō*.

Lesson Nineteen (135)

D. VERB SYNOPSIS

Do a verb synopsis of the third conjugation verb *regō, regere, rēxī, rēctum* in the present, imperfect, and future tenses, active voice, in the third person plural.

Present stem of *regō*: _____

TENSE	SYNOPSIS	TRANSLATION
Tense	Synopsis	Translation
present		
imperfect		
future		

E. DERIVATIVE DIGGING

Look up the English derivative *tangible*, write the definition on the lines below and give the Latin origin.

Definition of *tangible*:_____

_____

Latin Origin: _____

20 Lesson Twenty

A. THIRD CONJUGATION VERBS (PERFECT, PLUPERFECT & FUTURE PERFECT TENSES)

In the perfect, pluperfect, and future perfect tenses, third conjugation verbs are conjugated in the same way as first and second conjugation verbs. The endings for these tenses are added to the perfect stem which is found by removing the ending from the *third principal part of the verb*.

For example, the perfect stem for *ducō, dūcere, dūxī, ductum* is *dūx-*. Study the following paradigms in the active voice and highlight the verb endings:

PERFECT TENSE

dūxī — *I led, have led, did lead*	dūximus — *we led, have led, did lead*
dūxistī — *you led, have led, did lead*	dūxistis — *you (pl.) led, have led, did lead*
dūxit — *he, she, it led, has led, did lead*	dūxērunt — *they led, have led, did lead*

PLUPERFECT TENSE

dūxeram — *I had led*	dūxerāmus — *we had led*
dūxerās — *you had led*	dūxerātis — *you (pl.) had led*
dūxerat — *he, she, it had led*	dūxerant — *they had led*

FUTURE PERFECT TENSE

dūxerō — *I will have led*	dūxerimus — *we will have led*
dūxeris — *you will have led*	dūxeritis — *you (pl.) will have led*
dūxerit — *he, she, it will have led*	dūxerint — *they will have led*

B. THIRD CONJUGATION STEMS

Give the present and perfect stems for the third conjugation verbs below. One is done as an example.

VERB	PRESENT STEM	PERFECT STEM
1. carpō	*carp-*	*carps-*
2. surgō		
3. edō		
4. regō		
5. cognōscō		
6. tangō		
7. dīcō		

C. THIRD CONJUGATION VERB TRANSLATION

Translate the third conjugation verbs below. Underline endings and highlight verb stems. All six tenses are represented.

1. carpit _____

2. carpsit _____

3. cognōscunt _____

4. cognōvērunt _____

5. dūximus _____

6. dūcimus _____

7. surgitis _____

8. surgētis _____

9. surrēxistis _____

10. dīcis _____

11. dīcēs _____

12. dīcēbās _____

13. dīxistī _____

14. dūcam _____

D. VERB SYNOPSIS

Do a verb synopsis of the third conjugation verb *tangō, tangere, tetīgī, tactum* in the first person plural.

Tense	Synopsis	Translation
present		
imperfect		
future		
perfect		
pluperfect		
future perfect		

E. TRANSLATION: ENGLISH TO LATIN

1. Julia touched a dirt clod on the ground. _____

2. The horses had eaten the branch's leaves. _____

3. Claudia will have plucked the roses. _____

4. We did recognize Julius. _____

F. ETYMOLOGY

Look up the English word *cenacle* in an English dictionary and write its meaning on the lines below. Then write out the etymology of *cenacle*.

Definition: _____

_____

Etymology: _____

_____

VOCABULARY

Memorize the following vocabulary words, including the genitive and gender for nouns, and the four principal parts for verbs.

WORD	DERIVATIVE	TRANSLATION
1. senex, senis, *m.*	_____	*old man*
2. fōns, fontis, *m.*	_____	*fountain*
3. pater, patris, *m.*	_____	*father*
4. māter, matris, *f.*	_____	*mother*
5. filia, -ae, *f.*	_____	*daughter*
6. lapis, lapidis, *m.*	_____	*stone*
7. famēs, famis, *f.*	_____	*hunger*
8. pānis, pānis, *m.*	_____	*bread*
9. vestis, vestis, *f.*	_____	*clothing, garment*
10. fluvius, -ī, *m.*	_____	*river*
11. statua, -ae, *f.*	_____	*statue*
12. tactiō, tactiōnis, *f.*	_____	*a touch*
13. iugulum, -ī, *n.*	_____	*throat*
14. misericordia, -ae, *f.*	_____	*pity, mercy*

15. fluō, fluere, flūxī, fluxum _____ *flow*

16. pōnō, ponere, posuī, positum _____ *put, place*

17. offerō, offere, obtulī, oblātum _____ *offer*

18. avārus, -a, -um _____ *greedy*

19. mīser, mīsera, mīserum _____ *wretched, miserable*

20. trāns *(prep. with acc.)* _____ *over, across*

REVIEW WORDS

1. ā, ab *(prep. with abl.)*   *from, away from*
2. ad *(prep. with acc.)*   *to, toward, near, at*
3. aqua, -ae, *f.*   *water*
4. avāritia, -ae, *f.*   *greed*
5. currō, -ere, cucurrī, cursum   *run*
6. dēvorō, -āre, -āvī, -ātum   *swallow, devour*
7. ē, ex *(prep. with abl.)*   *out of, from*
8. fīlius, -ī, *m.*   *son*
9. in *(prep. with abl.)*   *in, on*
10. lavō, -āre, lāvi, lautum   *wash, bathe*
11. manus, -ūs, *f.*   *hand*
12. occultō, -āre, -āvī, -ātum   *hide*
13. piscis, -is, *m.*   *fish*
14. portō, -āre, -āvī, -ātum   *carry*
15. rēx, rēgis, *m.*   *king*
16. ululō, -āre, -āvī, -ātum   *howl, scream*
17. ambulō, -āre, -āvī, -ātum   *walk*
18. repente *(adv.)*   *suddenly*

21 Lesson Twenty-One

A. THIRD DECLENSION & THIRD DECLENSION I-STEM NOUNS

Third declension nouns behave somewhat differently from first and second declension nouns. Most significantly, the nominative singular endings can vary greatly. Although represented by *x*, other possible nominative singular endings include *-or*, *-ās*, *-ōs*, *-es*, *-is*, *-ō*, *-er*, *-ūs*, and *-al*. But all third declension nouns are identified by *-is* in the genitive singular. The base of the noun is found by removing the genitive singular ending.

While the gender of first, second, and second declension neuter nouns is usually obvious from the nominative singular ending (*-us* is masculine, *-a* is feminine, and *-um* is neuter), this is not true for third declension. It is necessary to memorize the gender of a third declension noun because of the many possibilities for *-x*.

Highlight the third declension noun chant endings on the example below.

THIRD DECLENSION EXAMPLE

Case	Singular	Plural
Nominative	rēx	rēgēs
Genitive	rēgis	rēgum
Dative	rēgī	rēgibus
Accusative	rēgem	rēgēs
Ablative	rēge	rēgibus

The third declension i-stem is a variation of regular third declension. The difference occurs in the genitive plural ending which is *-ium* instead of *-um*. There are three rules for identifying I-stem nouns, two of which will be discussed here. The third rule pertains to neuter nouns only and will be discussed later.

Rule #1: If the nominative singular ends in *-is* or *-ēs* and the genitive singular has the same number of syllables as the nominative, then the noun is an i-stem. *Famēs* is an example.

Rule #2: If the nominative singular ends in *-s* or *-x* and its base ends in two consonants, then the noun is an i-stem. *Fōns* is an example.

Highlight the third declension i-stem endings on the following example:

THIRD DECLENSION I-STEM EXAMPLE

Case	Singular	Plural
Nominative	famēs	famēs
Genitive	famis	famium
Dative	famī	famibus
Accusative	famem	fames
Ablative	fame	famibus

List two other third declension i-stem nouns from List 8.

_____

B. NOUN BASES

Give the base for the nouns below:

NOUN   **BASE**

1. rēx   _____

2. lapis   _____

3. tactiō   _____

C. TRANSLATION

Translate the sentences below. Especially watch for third declension nouns and third conjugation verbs.

1. Līberī trāns fluvium in lapidibus ambulāverant. _____

_____

2. Māter Claudiae cēnam dederat et Claudia properāvit ad fluvium. _____

_____

3. Fluvius cito flūxit sed Claudia aquam fluviī tetigit et potāvit. _____

_____

4. Claudia cēnam portāvit trāns fluvium. _____

_____

5. Repente, piscis magnus surrēxit et cēnam ē manū Claudiae carpsit. _____

_____

6. Claudia terrēbātur. _____

7. Claudia ululāvit et occultāvit inter lapidēs. _____

_____

8. Līberī ā flūviō cucurrērunt ad Claudiam miseram. _____

_____

9. Piscis magnus rīsit et cēnam dēvorāvit. _____

_____

10. Iūlia, Iūlius, et Claudius Claudiae cibum dedērunt. _____

_____

D. REVIEW

1. How do you recognize a third conjugation verb?_____

_____

_____

_____

_____

2. What case is used for possessive nouns? _____

3. How is a Latin adverb formed? _____

_____

4. What helping verb is used to translate the pluperfect tense? _____

E. TIDBIT

Iuppiter Lapis was a sacred stone upon which Romans could swear an oath. Because one of Jupiter's aspects was that of lawgiver, this stone represented Jupiter's authority. It was located in the temple of Jupiter.

22 Lesson Twenty-Two

A. THIRD DECLENSION NEUTER AND THIRD DECLENSION NEUTER I-STEM NOUNS

Two other neuter variations of third declension also exist. Like all neuter nouns, the nominative and accusative endings are the same. Examine the paradigm below for a regular third declension neuter noun. Then study the example, *caput* (*head*), a word we have learned in a previous book.

Third Declension Neuter

x	a
is	um
ī	ibus
x	a
e	ibus

Example:

caput	capita
capitis	capitum
capitī	capitibus
caput	capita
capite	capitibus

Now examine the third declension neuter i-stem paradigm and its example, *animal, animalis* (*animal*), also from a previous book. Circle the places where the i-stem neuter differs from the regular third declension neuter.

Third Declension Neuter I-Stem

x	ia
is	ium
ī	ibus
x	ia
ī	ibus

Example:

animal	animalia
animalis	animalium
animalī	animalibus
animal	animalia
animalī	animalibus

Memorize the following rule for recognizing third declension i-stem neuter nouns:

Rule #3

If a noun is neuter and ends in *-al* or *-e* in the nominative singular, then the noun is an i-stem.

N.B. As with second declension neuter nouns, third declension neuter and neuter i-stem nouns look the same in the nominative and accusative cases.

B. THIRD DECLENSION I-STEM REVIEW

Fill in the blanks for all three rules.

Rule #1: If the nominative singular ends in _____ or _____ and the genitive singular has the same number of _____ as the nominative, then the noun is an i-stem.

Rule #2: If the nominative singular ends in _____ or _____ and its base ends in

_____, then the noun is an i-stem.

Rule #3: If a noun is neuter and ends in _____ or _____ in the nominative singular,

then the noun is an i-stem.

C. NOUN-ADJECTIVE COMPOSITION

Translate the noun adjective phrases below into Latin. Be sure to translate the noun first, putting it into the case given. Make the adjective match the noun in gender, number, and case!

1. the greedy old men (accusative)   *senes avarōs* _____

2. the miserable daughter (nominative)   _____

3. the good fathers (dative)   _____

4. the golden animal (ablative)   _____

5. the proud king (ablative)   _____

6. the large stones (nominative)   _____

7. the long river (accusative) _____

8. the beautiful statue (dative) _____

D. CORRECTION AND TRANSLATION

Each of the Latin sentences below contain mistakes. Read the English translations and then write the correct Latin version of each sentence on the line, using a red pen.

1. Māter pānem edēbit. (one mistake) _____

   Translation: *Mother will eat bread.*

2. Fluviō trāns lapidem flūxit. (two mistakes) _____

   Translation: *The river flowed over the stones.*

3. Senex avārum argentum in arcam magnās posuerat. (three mistakes) _____

   _____

   Translation: *The greedy old man was putting silver into the large chest.*

Lesson Twenty-Two   149

23 Lesson Twenty-Three

A. CONJUGATION IDENTIFICATION

Identify whether the verbs below are first, second, or third conjugation.

VERB	CONJUGATION
1. fluō, fluere	_____
2. pōnō, pōnere	_____
3. pōtō, pōtāre	_____
4. rīdeō, rīdēre	_____
5. dīcō, dīcere	_____

B. FUTURE TENSE

Write out the *future tense* chants for first/second conjugation verbs and for third conjugation verbs.

FIRST/SECOND CONJUGATION

THIRD CONJUGATION

C. VERB TRANSLATION

Translate verbs from first, second, and third conjugations.

1. carpimus _____

2. carpsimus _____

3. carpēmus _____

4. ēdērunt _____

5. ēderint _____

6. ēderant _____

7. potābit _____

8. rīsit _____

9. rīdet _____

10. reget _____

11. regit _____

12. rēxit _____

D. THIRD DECLENSION CHANTS

Write out the third declension noun chants below from memory and then check your work.

THIRD DECLENSION

x	
is	

THIRD DECLENSION NEUTER

x	
is	

THIRD DECLENSION I-STEM			THIRD DECLENSION I-STEM NEUTER	
is			x	ia
is			is	

E. ABLATIVE OF PERSONAL AGENT

The *ablative of personal agent* is used with the preposition *ā, ab* and occurs when an action is accomplished by means of a person instead of an inanimate object or tool.

The *ablative of personal agent* is only used with *passive voice verbs*. Notice that *a, ab* means *by* when used with the ablative of personal agent. Study the examples below.

The wine was drunk by the old man.	*Vīnum potābātur ā sene.*
The food will be devoured by Julius.	*Cibus dēvorābitur ab Iūliō.*

N.B. Notice that *ā* is used in front of nouns beginning with a consonant and *ab* is used in front of nouns beginning with a vowel.

Practice translating the *ablative of personal agent* in the sentences below:

1. Cēna bona parābātur ā mātre Claudiae. _____

_____

2. Glēbae multae iactantur ā Sāxō et Claudiō. _____

_____

3. Arbor ornābitur ā patre, Iūliō, et Iūliā. _____

_____

Challenge question: What use of the ablative does the phrase *on the ground* exemplify?

_____

F. REVIEW

1. In addition to the *ablative of personal agent*, what are the other ablatives we have learned?

Ablative of _____

Ablative of _____

Ablative of _____

Ablative of _____

Ablative of _____

2. Translate the linking verbs below.

fuerant _____

erimus _____

es _____

fuistis _____

eram _____

fuerit _____

(24) Lesson Twenty-Four

King Midas and the Golden Touch

Translate the story of King Midās.

1. Sīlēnus, magister Bacchī, in asinō errāverat per terrās. _____

_____

2. Midās Rēx Sīlēnum et asinum cognōvit et eōs ad rēgiam apportāvit. _____

_____

3. Midās Sīlēnō cibum et vīnum dedit et senī hospitium mōnstrāvit. _____

_____

4. Tum Midās Rēx Sīlēnum ad Bacchum dūxit. _____

_____

5. Bacchus grātus erat et rēgī optātum obtulit. _____

_____

6. Midās Rēx avāritiam habēbat et aurum amābat. _____

_____

7. Igitur tactiōnem auream optāvit. _____

_____

8. Bacchus Midam monēbat dē perīculō sed Midās avārus aurum optāvit. _____

_____

_____

9. Statim, Midās Rēx rāmulum carpsit ā rāmō. _____

_____

10. Rāmulus erat aureus. _____

11. Fōlium in rāmulō erat aureum. _____

12. Lapidem habuit et lapis erat aureus! _____

_____

13. Midās rōsam tetīgit et erat rōsa aurea. _____

_____

14. Rēx laetus ad mensam sēdit et ēdit, et mensa et sella erant aureae. _____

_____

_____

15. Midās pānem ēdit sed pānis erat aurum; nōn potest cibum edere!_____

_____

16. Temptāvit vīnum potāre sed vīnum in iūgulō erat aurum! _____

_____

17. Postrēmō, fīlia rēgis cucurrit ad patrem et eum tetigit. _____

_____

18. Fīlia Midae erat statua aurea! _____

_____

19. Rēx mīser Bacchum implōrāvit eum servāre ā tactiōne aureā et fīliam reddere. _____

_____

_____

20. Bacchus Midam dīxit, "Lavā caput et corpus in Fluviō Pactolō ." _____

_____

21. Midās lāvit in fluviō et harēna fluviī erat aurea._____

_____

22. Tactiō Aurea erat in fluviō. _____

23. Omnia reddēbantur et Midās Rēx gaudēbat! _____

_____

GLOSSARY FOR MIDĀS RĒX ET TACTIO AUREA

1. asinus, -ī, *m.*   *donkey*
2. Bacchus, -ī, *m.*   *god of wine*
3. currō, -ere, cucurrī, cursum   *run*
4. eōs   *them (masc. acc. plural)*
5. errō, -āre, -āvī, -ātum   *wander*
8. eum   *him (mas. acc. sing.)*
9. et...et   *both...and*
10. gaudeo, -ēre, gāvīsus sum   *rejoice*
11. grātus, -a, -um   *grateful*
12. harēna, -ae, *f.*   *sand*
13. hospitium, -ī, *n.*   *hospitality*
14. igitur   *therefore*
15. laetus, -a, -um   *happy*
16. lavo, -āre, lāvī, lautum   *wash*
17. Midās Rēx   *King Midās*
18. offerō, offere, obtuli, oblātum   *offer*
19. omnia, -ium, *n.*   *all, everything*
20. Pactolus, -ī, *m.*   *a river in Lydia which was said to bring down golden sands*
21. per (*prep. with acc.*)   *through*
22. postrēmō   *finally*
23. reddō, -ere, reddīdī, reddītum   *restore*
24. sedeō, -ēre, sēdī, sessum   *sit*

Lesson Twenty-Four   157

25. sella, -ae, *f.*   *seat, chair*
26. servō, -āre, -āvī, -ātum   *save*
27. Sīlēnus, -ī, *m.*   *tutor and companion of Bacchus*
28. statim   *immediately*
29. tum   *then*

Unit Four Review

A. VERB REVIEW

Translate the verbs below and identify the conjugation and tense of each one. You may abbreviate. One is done as an example.

VERB	TRANSLATION	CONJ.	TENSE
1. carpsistis	*you (pl.) plucked (have plucked, did pluck)*	*3rd*	*perfect*
2. regēmus			
3. regimus			
4. surrēxit			
5. potāverint			
6. tangit			
7. tetigit			
8. rident			
9. ridēbunt			
10. dūcitis			
11. dūcētis			
12. dūxeritis			

B. VERB TRNALTION

Now translate these verbs into Latin. Use *dīcō* for 1–3.

1. you will tell   _____

2. you are telling   _____

3. you did tell   _____

4. they ate   _____

5. they will eat   _____

6. they eat   _____

C. VERB SYNOPSIS REVIEW

Do a synopsis of the third conjugation verb *cōgnōscō, cōgnōscere, cōgncōgnōscōvī, cōgnitum* in the third person singular, active voice.

Tense	Synopsis	Translation
present		
imperfect		
future		
perfect		
pluperfect		
future perfect		

Now do a synopsis of the first conjugation verb *ornō, -āre, -āvī, -ātum* in the third person singular, *passive voice.*

Tense	Synopsis	Translation
present		
imperfect		
future		

D. THIRD DECLENSION OMIT REVIEW

Decline the third declension nouns below:

THIRD DECLENSION

lapis	
lapidis	

THIRD DECLENSION I-STEM

pānis	
pānis	

THIRD DECLENSION NEUTER

caput	
capitis	

THIRD DECLENSION I-STEM NEUTER

mare	
maris	

E. THIRD DECLENSION RULES REVIEW

Complete the rules for identifying third declension nouns below:

Rule #1: If the nominative singular ends in _____ or _____ and the genitive singular

has the same number of _____ as the nominative, then the noun is an i-stem.

Rule #2: If the nominative singular ends in _____ or _____ and its base ends in

_____, then the noun is an i-stem.

Rule #3: If a noun is neuter and ends in _____ or _____ in the nominative singular,

then the noun is an i-stem.

Unit Four Review **161**

F. TRANSLATION

Translate the sentences below. Pay attention to endings and mentally label parts of speech. Consider whether verbs are from 1st / 2nd conjugations or 3rd conjugation! Watch for singular and plural endings. Sentence #6 is in English and must be translated into Latin.

1. Māter līberīs et Saxō cibum parāvit et cēnam magnam ēdērunt. _____

_____

2. Puerī ā mensā surrēxerant et properāvērunt ad fontem. _____

_____

3. Iūlius aquam potābit ā fonte et mātrī rōsās carpet. _____

_____

4. Iūlia et Claudia senem avārum cōgnōscunt. _____

_____

5. Senex avārus cibum multum ēderat et erat miser! _____

_____

6. The river will flow among the stones. _____

G. DERIVATIVE REVIEW

List ten derivatives and their Latin origins from Lists 7 and 8.

DERIVATIVE	LATIN ORIGIN
1. _____	_____
2. _____	_____
3. _____	_____
4. _____	_____

5. _____   _____

6. _____   _____

7. _____   _____

8. _____   _____

9. _____   _____

10. _____   _____

Unit 5

9 List Nine

VOCABULARY

Memorize the following Latin words and their translations.

WORD	DERIVATIVE	TRANSLATION
1. labyrinthus, -ī, *m.*	_____	*labyrinth*
2. carcer, carceris, *m.*	_____	*prison*
3. turris, -is, *f.*	_____	*tower*
4. gavia, -ae, *f.*	_____	*seagull*
5. avis, -is, *f.*	_____	*bird*
6. pinna, -ae, *f.*	_____	*feather*
7. cōgitātiō, cōgitatiōnis, *f.*	_____	*idea*
8. lītus, litōris, *n.*	_____	*seashore*
9. mare, maris, *n.*	_____	*sea*
10. īnsula, -ae, *f.*	_____	*island*
11. corpus, corporis, *n.*	_____	*body*
12. scandō, -ere, scandī, scansum	_____	*climb*
13. fugiō, -ere, fūgī, fugitum	_____	*flee from*
14. volō, -āre, -āvī, -ātum	_____	*fly*
15. aedificō, -āre, -āvī, -ātum	_____	*build*

16. adfīgō, adfīgere, adfīxī, adfīxum   _____   *fasten to, affix*

17. capiō, -ere, cēpī, captum   _____   *capture*

18. faciō, -ere, fēcī, factum   _____   *make*

19. liquefaciō, -facere, -fēcī, -factum   _____   *melt*

20. prope *(prep. with acc.)*   _____   *near*

REVIEW WORDS

1. aedificium, -ī, *n.*   *building*
2. aer, aeris, *m.*   *air*
3. ala, -ae, *f.*   *wing*
4. arca, -ae, *f.*   *box, chest*
5. castellum, -i, *n.*   *castle*
6. fabricō, -āre, -āvī, -ātum   *form, forge, shape, make*
7. legō, -ere, lēgī, lectum   *gather, collect*
8. levō, -āre, -āvī, -ātum   *lift*
9. ligō, -āre, -āvī, -ātum   *tie, bind*
10. moveō, -ēre, movī, motum   *move*
11. operculum, -ī, *n.*   *lid*
12. per *(prep. with acc.)*   *through*
13. propero, -āre, -āvī, -ātum   *hurry, hasten*
14. scopulus, -ī, *m.*   *cliff*
15. scorpius, -ī, *m.*   *scorpion*
16. sōl, sōlis, *m.*   *sun*
17. stola, -ae, *f.*   *dress*
18. videō, -ēre, vīdī, vīsum   *see*

25 Lesson Twenty-Five

A. DIRECT QUESTIONS

In this lesson we will learn three ways to ask a direct question in Latin. The first type of question is the most basic and simply seeks information. To form this type of question, *-ne* is added to the end of the *first word* in the sentence. Frequently, the first word in a Latin question is the verb.

Study the examples below:

Volāvitne avis?	*Did the bird fly?* or *Has the bird flown?*
Aedificabuntne līberī labyrinthum?	*Will the children build a labyrinth?*
Esne dēfessus?	*Are you tired?*

Notice that the English translations begin with a helping verb which belongs to a particular verb tense. The first example is from the perfect tense, the second from the future, and the third from the present.

A second type of question could be called a *leading question.* This question expects a *yes* answer and begins the question with the interrogative particle *nonne.* For example:

Nonne avis volāvit?	*The bird did fly, didn't it? (did it not?)*

Notice that the first statement is positive and the negative adverb *not* appears after the comma.

A third type of question expects a *no* answer and begins with the interrogative particle *num.*

Num avis volāvit?	*The bird didn't (did not) fly, did it?*

This time the first part of the sentence contains the negative *not.*

N.B. Both *nonne* and *num* **expect** a particular answer even if that answer is not given. In the *nonne* question above the person asking the question expects that the bird did fly (even if it didn't). In the *num* question, the person asking expects that the bird did not fly (even if it did).

THIRD CONJUGATION I-STEM VERBS

Third conjugation i-stem verbs vary from regular third conjugation verbs because the present stem, which is found by removing the *-ō* from the first principal part of the verb, ends in *-ī*.

Consider the verb *capiō, capere, cēpī, captum.* If we remove the *-ō* from *capiō (capture)* the present stem is *capi-* and the endings are put on that stem. Study the present, imperfect, and future tense examples of *capiō* which use the present stem.

N.B. The "i" of the present stem only appears in *capiō* and *capiunt* in the present tense.

PRESENT

capiō — *I capture*	capimus — *we capture*
capis — *you capture*	capitis — *you (pl.) capture*
capit — *he, she, it captures*	capiunt — *they capture*

IMPERFECT

capiēbam — *I was capturing*	capiēbāmus — *we were capturing*
capiēbās — *you were capturing*	capiēbātis — *you (pl.) were capturing*
capiēbat — *he, she, it was capturing*	capiēbant — *they were capturing*

FUTURE

capiam — *I will capture*	capiēmus — *we will capture*
capiēs — *you will capture*	capiētis — *you (pl.) will capture*
capiet — *he, she, it will capture*	capient — *they will capture*

The perfect, pluperfect, and future perfect tenses in the active voice all add endings to the perfect stem, which is formed from the third principal part in the same way as other conjugations:

PERFECT

cēpī — *I captured*	cēpimus — *we captured*
cēpistī — *you captured*	cēpistis — *you (pl.) captured*
cēpit — *he, she, it captured*	cēpērunt — *they captured*

PLUPERFECT

cēperam — *I had captured*	cēperāmus — *we had captured*
cēperās — *you had captured*	cēperātis — *you (pl.) had captured*
cēperat — *he, she, it had captured*	cēperant — *they had captured*

FUTURE PERFECT

cēperō — *I will have captured*	cēperimus — *we will have captured*
cēperis — *you will have captured*	cēperitis — *you (pl.) will have captured*
cēperit — *he, she, it will have captured*	cēperint — *they will have captured*

B. QUESTION TRANSLATION

Translate the questions below. Be sure to use the correct helping verb in your question. Some sentences contain third conjugation or third conjugation i-stem verbs. Remember that third conjugation verbs look different from first and second conjugation verbs in the present, future, and imperfect tenses!

1. Capietne Iūlia gaviam? _____

2. Volābitne gāvia? _____

3. Adfigēbantne Claudia et Iūlia pinnās in stolīs? _____

_____

4. Nonne Claudius pinnās legit in litōre? _____

_____

5. Num Claudius pinnās legit in litōre? _____

_____

Challenge question: Aedificāverimusne turrem in īnsulā? _____

_____

C. QUESTION TRANSLATION

Translate these direct questions into Latin. The helping verb tells you what verb tense to use.

1. Will Julius flee from the large bird? _____

_____

2. Did the wings lift the bird's body into the air? _____

_____

3. Had Claudia and Julia made a castle on the seashore? _____

_____

4. Claudius is not building the girls a tower, is he? _____

_____

5. Saxum was hurrying through the labyrinth, wasn't he? _____

_____

D. ETYMOLOGY

Give the etymology for the word *incarcerate.* Then write the definition of the word. Correctly use the word *incarcerate* in a sentence.

Etymology: _____

_____

Definition: _____

Sentence: _____

_____

_____

 Lesson Twenty-Five

(26) Lesson Twenty-Six

A. QUESTION REVIEW

Fill in the blanks about direct questions in Latin which use *-ne, nonne,* and *num.*

To form a simple question in Latin, add _____ to the _____ word in the sentence.

What part of speech is usually used with this ending? _____

When expecting a *yes* answer, begin a question with _____ .

When expecting a *no* answer, begin a question with _____ .

B. SYNOPSIS

Do a synopsis of the third conjugation i-stem verb *faciō, facere, fēcī, factum* in the third person singular.

TENSE	SYNOPSIS	TRANSLATION
present		
imperfect		
future		
perfect		
pluperfect		
future perfect		

C. THIRD CONJUGATION I-STEM TRANSLATION

Translate the third conjugation i-stem verbs below. Underline those verbs which contain the extra *i*.

1. fūgit _____

2. fugit _____

3. fugiet _____

4. fugiēbat _____

5. facimus _____

6. faciēmus _____

7. fēcimus _____

8. fēcerāmus _____

9. fēcerimus _____

10. capiō _____

11. capiam _____

12. cēpēro _____

D. QUESTION TRANSLATION

Review the explanation of direct questions at the beginning of Lesson 25. Then translate the sets of questions below containing *-ne, nonne,* and *num.*

SET #1

a. Fugietne gāvia scorpium? _____

_____

b. Nonne gāvia scorpium fugiet?_____

_____

c. Num gāvia scorpium fugiet? _____

_____

a. Volāveruntne aves ad mare? _____

_____

b. Nonne avēs ad mare volāverunt? _____

_____

c. Num avēs ad mare volāverunt? _____

_____

Challenge: Identify the declension for each of the nouns below:

NOUN   **DECLENSION**

1. lītus, lītoris, n.   _____

2. mare, maris, n.   _____

3. corpus, corpōris, n.   _____

10 List Ten

A. VOCABULARY

Memorize the following Latin words and their translations.

1. bracchium, -ī, *n.* _____ *arm*

2. līnea, -ae, *f.* _____ *thread*

3. cēra, -ae, *f.* _____ *wax*

4. calor, calōris, *m.* _____ *heat*

5. gaudium, -ī, *n.* _____ *joy, happiness*

6. templum, -ī, *n.* _____ *temple*

7. mors, mortis, *f.* _____ *death*

8. clamō, -āre, -āvī, -ātum _____ *shout*

9. doceō, -ēre, docuī, doctum* _____ *teach*

10. cadō, -ere, cecīdī, casum _____ *fall, drop*

11. flūtō, -āre, -āvī, -ātum _____ *float*

12. maneō, -ēre, mansī, mansum _____ *remain*

13. lūgeō, -ēre, lūxī, ---------- _____ *mourn*

14. ubi _____ *where*

15. quid _____ *what*

* *The verb doceo is unusual because the indirect object is put into the accusative case instead of the dative case!*

16. quis   _____   *who*

17. quot   _____   *how many*

18. quandō   _____   *when*

19. tūtus, -a, -um   _____   *safe*

20. circā *(prep. with acc.)* _____   *around*

REVIEW WORDS

1. ad *(prep. with acc.)*   *to, toward*
2. aeger, aegra, aegrum   *sick*
3. aer, aeris, *m.*   *air*
4. altus, -a, -um   *high, tall*
5. aqua, -ae, *f.*   *water*
6. curō, currere, cucurrī, cursum   *run*
7. dē *(prep. with abl.)*   *down from, about, concerning*
8. discipulus, -ī, *m.*   *(male) student*
9. hōra, -ae, *f.*   *hour*
10. īra, -ae, *f.*   *anger*
11. liber, -brī, *m*   *book*
12. ludus, -ī, *m.*   *school, game*
13. mūrus, -ī, *m.*   *wall*
14. tabula, -ae, *f.*   *board*
15. terra, -ae, *f.*   *land, earth*
16. vestis, vestis, *f.*   *clothing, garment*

ORDINAL NUMBERS

prīmus, -a, -um	*first*		sextus, -a, -um	*sixth*
secundus, -a, -um	*second*		septimus, -a, -um	*seventh*
tertius, -a, -um	*third*		octāvus, -a, -um	*eighth*
quartus, -a, -um	*fourth*		nōnus, -a, -um	*ninth*
quīntus, -a, -um	*fifth*		decimus, -a, -um	*tenth*

(27) Lesson Twenty-Seven

A. MORE ON QUESTIONS

Questions can also be formed with specific "question words". Study the examples below.

Ubi est Iūlia?	*Where is Julia?*
Quid facitis?	*What are you making?*
Quot pinnās lēgit Claudia?	*How many feathers did Claudia gather?*

B. QUESTION TRANSLATION

Translate these questions into English.

1. Quot pinnās gāvia habet? _____

_____

2. Quis erat rēx terrae? _____

3. Quid flūtābat in marī? _____

4. Quandō puerī et puellae turrem in lītōre aedificābunt? _____

_____

5. Ubi līberī et Saxum ambulāverant? _____

_____

C. ANSWER COMPOSITION

Write your own *Latin* answers to the questions in part B! For number questions, refer to the cardinal numbers *unus, duo, trēs, quattuor, quinque, sex, septem, octo, novem, decem, centum, mille.*

Unus, duo, and *trēs* must match the nouns they describe in gender, number and case.* The other numbers do not decline. For "when" questions, refer to the List Ten Review Words to review the ordinal numbers and pair them with the Latin noun *hōra,* which means *hour* in the ablative case.

1. _____

2. _____

3. _____

4. _____

5. _____

	Masculine	Feminine	Neuter
Nominative	unus	una	unum
Accusative	unum	unam	unum
Nominative	duo	duae	duo
Accusative	duos	duas	duo
Nominative	trēs	trēs	tria
Accusative	trēs	trēs	tria

---

*   *The Latin numbers for one, two, and three are declined below in the nominative and accusative cases.*

D. QUESTION TRANSLATION

Translate these questions into Latin:

1. Does the sun's heat melt the wax? _____

_____

2. Will the birds fly into the air? _____

_____

3. Was Saxum fleeing into the labyrinth? _____

_____

4. Claudius is building a wall, isn't he? _____

_____

5. Claudius is not building a wall, is he? _____

_____

28 Lesson Twenty-Eight

A. COMMANDS, VOCATIVE CASE

To form Latin commands (or imperatives) for first or second conjugation verbs to one person, remove the *-re* ending from the second principal part of the verb. This is also how we find the present stem of the verb as explained in Lesson 1. Remember that the implied subject of a command is *you* or *you all*. Consider the examples below:

| Amā Deum. | *Love God.* |
| Movē mensam. | *Move the table.* |

To make a command to more than one person add *-te* to the verb stem:

| Amāte Deum. | *Love God.* |
| Movēte mensam. | *Move the table.* |

To form a singular command in the third conjugation remove the *-ō* from the first principal part of the verb and add *-e to the stem*. For third conjugation i-stem verbs, remove the *-iō* of the first principal part and then add *-e* to the stem. See the examples:

| Cade lapidem. | *Drop the rock.* |
| Cape pīlam | *Catch a ball.* |

To make a command to more than one person add *-ite* to the present stem.

| Cadite lapidēs. | *Throw the balls.* |
| Capite pīlās. | *Catch balls.* |

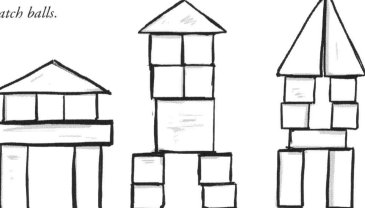

VOCATIVE CASE

The vocative case is used to speak to someone directly. It is used with the second person and is usually set apart by commas. The endings for the vocative case are the same as the nominative with the exception of second declension singular nouns which end in -us or -ius. Nouns ending in -us use -e as the vocative ending. Nouns ending in -ius have -ī as the vocative ending. Vocative plurals always use the nominative plural endings.

Es pulchra, Iūlia.	*Julia, you are beautiful.*
Eras āeger, Marce.	*Mark, you were sick.*
Eris tūtus, Claudī.	*Claudius (Claude), you will be safe.*

The vocative case is frequently paired with a command. When that happens, the command usually appears first, followed by the vocative. Study the following examples:

Amāte, puellae, Deum.	*Girls, love God.*
Movē, amīce, mensam.	*Friend, move the table.*
Portā, Iulī, sellam.	*Julius, carry the chair.*

B. IMPERATIVE AND VOCATIVE TRANSLATION

Translate the sentences below. Some contain imperatives and some contain vocatives as well.

1. Flūtate in aquā._____

2. Manē, Iūlī, in īnsulā. _____

3. Fugite, puellae, pērīculum. _____

4. Curre, discipule, ad ludum. _____

5. Estis citī, līberī._____

6. Fuistī aeger, Claudī. _____

7. Ambulābisne, Claudia, inter lapidēs?_____

_____

8. Iactāte, gāviae, pinnās. _____

C. TRANSLATION: ENGLISH TO LATIN.

1. Julius, carry the books. _____

2. Students, look at the board. _____

3. Mother, will you prepare dinner? _____

4. Son, drop the dirt clod. _____

5. Men, make a wall around the prison. _____

_____

D. VERB SYNOPSIS

Do a synopsis of the third conjugation i-stem verb *faciō, facere, fēcī, factum* in the second person plural, active voice.

TENSE	SYNOPSIS	TRANSLATION
present		
imperfect		
future		
perfect		
pluperfect		
future perfect		

Do a synopsis of the first conjugation verb *aedificō, -āre, -āvī, -ātum* in the second person plural, passive voice.

TENSE	SYNOPSIS	TRANSLATION
present		
imperfect		
future		

E. TIDBIT

In ancient Rome, there were only about eighteen first names used for boys because the Romans named boys after male relatives. Girls were not given first names but went by the feminine form of the family name. If the family name was *Julius*, the daughters would be known as *Julia*. If there were several daughters they might have nicknames, or even numbers, to distinguish them.

29 Lesson Twenty-Nine

A. ABLATIVE OF MANNER

The way in which an action is done is put in the ablative case
with the preposition *cum*. Study the examples below:

> Iūlia et Claudia dōna apportāverant cum gaudiō.
> *Julia and Claudia had brought the gifts with joy.*

> Iuppiter fulmen iactāvit cum īrā.
> *Jupiter threw the thunderbolt with anger.*

Choose from these nouns to help translate sentences containing the ablative of manner:

> gaudium *(joy)*, īra *(anger)*, avāritia *(greed)*, invidia *(envy)*, malevolentia *(spite, malice)*,
> benevolentia *(good will, kindness)*, misericordia *(pity, mercy)*

1. Uxor puerō pānem et vestem cum misericordiā dābat. _____

_____

2. Senex argentum et aurum in arcā cum avāritiā occultāvit. _____

_____

3. Rēx virōs vocābit cum beneficiō._____

_____

4. Nōn capiēbāmus gāviās cum malevolentiā._____

_____

B. QUESTION TRANSLATION

Translate the questions below.

1. Fugiēbantne gāviae vulturiōs? _____

2. Nonne virī turrem altam aedificābunt prope labyrinthum? _____

_____

3. Num Iūlia arcam ligāvit līneā? _____

_____

4. Quid ceciderat in mare? _____

5. Quīs manēbit in lītore? _____

6. Quot templa sunt in Rōmā? _____

7. Quandō calor sōlis cēram liquefaciet? _____

8. Did the birds fly around the tower? _____

C. NOUN-ADJECTIVE TRANSLATION

Translate these noun-adjective phrases into Latin. Put them in the nominative case.

1. one girl   _____

   two girls   _____

   three girls   _____

2. one boy   _____

   two boys   _____

   three boys   _____

3. one rock   _____

   two rocks   _____

   three rocks   _____

30 Lesson Thirty
Daedalus and Icarus

Translate the story of *Daedalus and Īcarus*.

1. Ōlim Daedalus Minoī, rēgī Cretae, labyrinthum aedificāvit. _____

_____

2. Sed rēx benevolentiam ā Daedalō remōvit et Daedalum et fīlium in carcere posuit. _____

_____

_____

3. Carcer turris alta in īnsulā erat. _____

_____

4. Daedalus et fīlius, Īcarus, poterant turrem fugere sed nōn poterant insulam fugere. _____

_____

_____

5. Daedalus cōgitātiōnem habuit. _____

6. Daedalus fīliō dīxit, "Minōs Rēx terram et mare regit, sed aerem non regit." _____

_____

_____

7. Daedalus et Īcarus gāviārum pinnās multās lēgērunt prope lītus et Daedalus sibi et Īcarō alās magnās

fēcit. _____

_____

8. Adfīxit pinnās ad alās cērā et līneā. _____

_____

9. Daedalus Īcarum docuit volāre. _____

10. Daedalus fīlium monuit, "Nē scande prope sōlem. Manē prope mē et tūtus eris."_____

_____

_____

11. Volāvērunt ab īnsulā in aerem. _____

_____

12. Sed Īcarus patrem nōn auscultāvit et subvolāvit ad sōlem._____

_____

13. Calor sōlis cēram liquefaciēbat et pinnae ab alīs cadēbant. _____

_____

_____

14. Īcarus alās movēbat sed nūllae pinnae manēbant. _____

_____

15. Puer in mare cecidit._____

16. Daedalus clāmābat et fīlium vocābat, "Īcare, ubi es?" _____

_____

17. Pinnae in aquā flūtābant et Daedalus corpus fīlī vīdit. _____

_____

18. Daedalus fīlium lugēbat et corpus Īcarī humāvit. _____

_____

19. Terra "Īcaria" vocābātur ā Daedalō. _____

_____

GLOSSARY

1. auscultō, -āre, -āvī, -ātum — *listen to*
2. Daedalus, -ī, *m.* — *mythical Athenian craftsman who built the Cretan labyrinth*
3. humō, -āre, -āvī, -ātum — *bury*
4. Īcarus, -ī. *m.* — *son of Daedalus*
5. Minōs, Minois, *m.* — *King of Crete*
6. nūllus, -a, -um — *no*
7. poterant — *they were able (form of "possum")*
8. regō, -ere, rēxī, rēctum — *rule*
9. removeō, -ēre, -mōvī, -motum — *remove*
10. sibi — *himself*
11. subvolō, -āre, -āvī, -ātum — *fly up*

A. VERB REVIEW

Write out the missing principal parts and translations from memory for the verbs below from Lists 9 and 10. Then check your answers and correct in red.

1ST	2ND	3RD	4TH	TRANSLATION
fugiō			fugitum	
	volāre			fly
		adfīxī		
capiō			captum	
	facere			make
lugeō		lūxī		
maneō			mansum	
	flūtāre			float
		cecidī		
doceō			doctum	

B. NOUN REVIEW

Write out the genitive, gender, and translation from memory for each of the nouns below from Lists 9 and 10. Then check your answers and correct in red.

NOUN	GENITIVE	GENDER	TRANSLATION
1. labyrinthus	_____	_____	_____
2. carcer	_____	_____	_____
3. lītus	_____	_____	_____

Unit Five Review   193

4. mare _____ ___ _____

5. corpus _____ ___ _____

6. bracchium _____ ___ _____

7. calor _____ ___ _____

8. cēra _____ ___ _____

9. gaudium _____ ___ _____

10. turris _____ ___ _____

C. VERB SYNOPSIS REVIEW

Do a verb synopsis for the second conjugation verb *doceō, docēre, docuī, doctum (teach)* in the first person plural, passive voice.

TENSE	SYNOPSIS	TRANSLATION
present		
imperfect		
future		

Do a verb synopsis for the third conjugation i-stem verb *fugiō, fugere, fūgī, fugitum* (flee from) in the first person plural, active voice.

TENSE	SYNOPSIS	TRANSLATION
present		
imperfect		
future		
perfect		
pluperfect		
future perfect		

D. QUESTION TRANSLATION REVIEW

Translate the questions below.

1. Docēbitne magistra līberōs* fābulās?_____

_____

2. Ceciditne Īcarus in mare? _____

3. Nonne Daedalus pinnās alīs adfīxerat? _____

_____

4. Num Īcarus Daedalum auscultābat? _____

_____

5. Ubi Īcarus volābit? _____

6. Quis manēbit in īnsulā? _____

* *Remember that the verb doceo puts both direct objects and indirect objects in the accusative case.*

E. IMPERATIVE AND VOCATIVE REVIEW

Translate these commands containing vocative nouns into Latin.

1. Julius and Claudius, build towers. _____

2. Marcus, remain on the island. _____

3. Girls, drop the feathers. _____

F. ABLATIVE TRANSLATION

Translate the sentences below and identify the type of ablative being used. Ablatives are in italics

Possible ablatives are: *time when, time during, place where, place from which, personal agent, means,* and *manner.*

1. Iūlia et Saxum *ā templo* ad turrem ambulant. _____

_____

Ablative: _____

2. Īcarus lūgēbātur *ā Daedalo.* _____

_____

Ablative: _____

3. Clamāvimus *cum gaudiō.* _____

Ablative: _____

4. Claudia stolam fabricāverat *lineā.* _____

_____

Ablative: _____

5. Gāviae ad turrem volāvērunt *septimā hōrā.* _____

_____

Ablative: _____

G. DERIVATIVE REVIEW

Choose five derivatives from Lists 9 and 10 and correctly use them in a short paragraph. Underline the derivatives used.

_____

_____

_____

_____

_____

_____

Unit 6

11 List Eleven

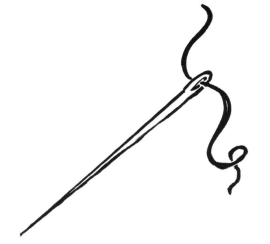

VOCABULARY

Memorize the following Latin words and their translations.

WORD	DERIVATIVE	TRANSLATION
1. metus, -ūs, *m.*	_____	*fear*
2. fructus, -ūs, *m.*	_____	*fruit*
3. sapientia, -ae, *f.*	_____	*wisdom*
4. ars, artis, *f.*	_____	*skill*
5. acus, -ūs, *f.*	_____	*needle*
6. dea, -ae, *f.*	_____	*goddess*
7. virgō, virginis, *f.*	_____	*maiden*
8. manus, -ūs, *f.*	_____	*hand*
9. adventus, -ūs, *m.*	_____	*arrival, approach*
10. exitus, -ūs, *m.*	_____	*departure, outcome*
11. usus, -ūs, *m.*	_____	*use, practice, experience*
12. textum, -ī, *n.*	_____	*cloth*
13. lāna, -ae, *f.*	_____	*wool*
14. texō, -ere, texuī, textum	_____	*weave*
15. neō, nēre, nēvī, nētum	_____	*spin*

16. contendō, -ere, contendī, contentum _____ *contend, compete*

17. audeō, -ēre, ausus sum* _____ *dare*

18. prōvocō, -āre, -āvī, -ātum _____ *challenge*

19. acūtus, -a, -um _____ *sharp*

20. perītus, -a, -um _____ *skillful*

REVIEW WORDS

1. adfīgō, -ere, -fīxī, -fīxum   *affix, attach*
2. amīca, -ae, f.   *female friend*
3. amīcus, -ī, m.   *male friend*
4. dēmōnstrō, -āre, -āvī, -ātum   *demonstrate, show*
5. diū   *for a long time*
6. doceō, -ēre, docuī, doctum   *teach*
7. exspectō, -āre, -āvī, -ātum   *wait for, expect*
8. faciō, -ere, fēcī, factum   *make*
9. fīlia, -ae, f.   *daughter*
10. habeō, -ēre, -uī, -itum   *have, hold*
11. Iuppiter, Iōvis, m.   *Jupiter*
12. moneō, -ēre, -uī, -itum   *warn*
13. multus, -a, -um   *much, many*
14. pulcher, pulchra, pulchrum   *beautiful, handsome*
15. quod   *because*
16. stola, -ae, f.   *dress*
17. sum, esse, fuī, futūrum   *be*

* *Audeo does not have four principal parts. You will only need to use the first and second principal parts in this book.*

31 Lesson Thirty-One

A. FOURTH DECLENSION NOUNS

Fourth declension nouns end in -*us* in the nominative singular and -*us* in the genitive singular. Because the nominative singular form of second declension nouns also ends in -*us* it is extremely important to pay close attention to the genitive forms. Study the paradigms below and note the differences between fourth declension and second declension.

FOURTH DECLENSION

us	ūs
ūs	uum
uī	ibus
um	ūs
ū	ibus

SECOND DECLENSION

us	ī
ī	ōrum
ō	īs
um	ōs
ō	īs

Here is an example of a fourth declension noun. Highlight the noun endings.

manus	manūs
manūs	manuum
manuī	manibus
manum	manūs
manū	manibus

Practice declining the fourth declension noun *acus*.

B. NOUN PRACTICE

Give the correct forms of the nouns below. Then write the declension of each noun on the next blank.

	NOUN FORM	DECLENSION
1. *adventus* in the accusative singular	_____	_____
2. *ars* in the nominative plural	_____	_____
3. *exitus* in the genitive singular	_____	_____
4. *dea* in the accusative plura	_____	_____
5. *fructus* in the dative singular	_____	_____
6. *virgō* in the ablative singular	_____	_____

C. TRANSLATION

Translate the sentences below.

1. Claudia Iūliae stolam faciēbat acū. _____

_____

2. Claudia artem multam dēmōnstrāvit quod usum multum habuit. _____

_____

3. Manus Claudiae acum acutum habēbat. _____

_____

4. Claudia lānam nēbat et textum pulchrum texēbat. _____

_____

5. Claudia est perīta! _____

D. SYNOPSIS

Do a synopsis of the second conjugation verb *neō, nēre, nēvī, nētum* in the second person plural.

TENSE	SYNOPSIS	TRANSLATION
present		
imperfect		
future		
perfect		
pluperfect		
future perfect		

E. DERIVATIVE DIGGING

Another derivative for the word *sapientia* (wisdom) is *sapid*. Look up this derivative in a dictionary and write both meanings below.

Sapid:

1. _____

_____

2. _____

_____

32 Lesson Thirty-Two

A. DEMONSTRATIVE ADJECTIVE *HIC, HAEC, HOC*

Demonstrative adjectives point out a person or thing and can be used as an adjective or a pronoun. Like other adjectives, demonstratives must match the noun they describe in gender, number, and case. The *hic, haec, hoc* chant means *this* in the singular and *these* in the plural and indicates a noun which is near the speaker.

Study the paradigm of *hic, haec, hoc* below.

SINGULAR (THIS)

CASE	MASCULINE	FEMININE	NEUTER
Nominative	hic	haec	hoc
Genitive	huius	huius	huius
Dative	huic	huic	huic
Accusative	hunc	hanc	hoc
Ablative	hōc	hāc	hōc

PLURAL (THESE)

CASE	MASCULINE	FEMININE	NEUTER
Nominative	hī	hae	haec
Genitive	hōrum	hārum	hōrum
Dative	hīs	hīs	hīs
Accusative	hōs	hās	haec
Ablative	hīs	hīs	hīs

Consider these nominative singular examples:

Masculine	Feminine	Neuter
hic puer — *this boy*	haec puella — *this girl*	hoc saxum — *this rock*

Now look at a sentence which uses these phrases in different cases:

(Nom.)   (Dat.)   (Acc.)

Hic puer huic puellae hoc saxum dat.   *This boy gives this girl this rock.*

Now look over these same examples in the plural.

Masculine	Feminine	Neuter
hī puerī — *these boys*	hae puellae — *these girls*	haec saxa — *these rocks*

(Nom.)   (Dat.)   (Acc.)

Hī puerī hīs puellīs haec saxa dant.   *These boys give these girls these rocks.*

N.B. Unlike many Latin adjectives, the demonstrative adjective precedes the noun it describes.

B. DEMONSTRATIVE ADJECTIVE PRACTICE

Translate the noun-adjective phrases below according to the formulas given. One is done as an example.

1. this skill (accusative singular)   *hanc artem*

2. this hand's (genitive singular)   _____

3. these arrivals (nominative plural)   _____

4. this experience (ablative singular)   _____

5. these departures (dative plural)   _____

6. this wool (nominative singular)   _____

7. these goddesses (accusative plural)   _____

8. these needles' (genitive plural)   _____

C. TRANSLATION: ENGLISH TO LATIN

Translate the sentences below into Latin. Be sure to make the demonstrative adjectives match the nouns they describe in gender, number, and case.

1. Julia gives this (female) friend this needle. _____

_____

2. Saxum had woven this cloth for Claudius. _____

_____

3. This skillful maiden did make Julia this dress with (by means of) this wool. _____

_____

4. These children were waiting for the arrival of these kings. _____

_____

D. VERB PRACTICE

Translate the verbs below and identify the conjugation and tense of each. One is done as an example.

VERB	CONJUGATION	TENSE	TRANSLATION
1. contendunt	*third*	*present*	*they compete, contend*
2. contendent	_____	_____	_____
3. contendērunt	_____	_____	_____
4. audet	_____	_____	_____
5. texet	_____	_____	_____
6. texuit	_____	_____	_____
7. texit	_____	_____	_____
8. nēmus	_____	_____	_____

9. nēverāmus   _____   _____   _____

10. prōvocābis   _____   _____   _____

E. ETYMOLOGY

Write out the etymology for the English derivative *sapient*.

_____

_____

12 List Twelve

A. VOCABULARY

Memorize the following Latin words and their translations.

WORD	DERIVATIVE	TRANSLATION
1. tēla, -ae, *f.*	_____	*web, loom*
2. arānea, -ae, *f.*	_____	*spider*
3. vetula, -ae, *f.*	_____	*old woman*
4. cōnsilium, -ī, *n.*	_____	*advice, plan*
5. celeritās, celeritātis, *f.*	_____	*speed*
6. color, colōris, *m.*	_____	*color*
7. superbia, -ae, *f.*	_____	*pride*
8. occāsus, -ūs, *m.*	_____	*downfall*
9. offensa, -ae, *f.*	_____	*displeasure*
10. peccātum, -ī, *n.*	_____	*sin, error*
11. simulō, -āre, -āvī, -ātum	_____	*pretend*
12. mutō, -āre, -āvī, -ātum	_____	*change*
13. caeruleus, -a, -um	_____	*blue*
14. ruber, rubra, rubrum	_____	*red*
15. flāvus, -a, -um	_____	*yellow*

List Twelve 211

16. viridis, viride   _____   *green*

17. stultus, -a, -um   _____   *foolish*

18. cornū, -ūs, *n.*   _____   *horn (animal or trumpet)*

19. genū, -ūs, *n.*   _____   *knee*

20. propter *(prep. with acc.)*   _____   *because of, on account of*

REVIEW WORDS

1. acūtus, -a, -um   *sharp*
2. aedificium, -ī, *n.*   *building*
3. auscultō, -āre, -āvī, -ātum   *listen to*
4. avia, -ae, *f.*   *grandmother*
5. bēstiola, -ae, *f.*   *insect*
6. canō, -ere, cecinī, cantum   *play (on an instrument; used with ablative)*
7. doceō, -ēre, -uī, doctum   *teach*
8. gladius, -ī, *m.*   *sword*
9. inlaqueō, -āre, -āvī, -ātum   *entrap*
10. līnea, -ae, *f.*   *thread*
11. magnus, -a, -um   *large, great*
12. mīles, militis, *m.*   *soldier*
13. multus, -a, -um   *much, many*
14. nuntiō, -āre, -āvī, -ātum   *announce*
15. parvus, -a, -um   *small*
16. pīla, -ae, *f.*   *ball*
17. pugnō, -āre, -āvī, -ātum   *fight*
18. rēx, rēgis, *m.*   *king*
19. spectō, -āre, -āvī, -ātum   *watch, look at*
20. sum, esse, fuī, futūrum   *be (esse=to be)*
21. textum, -ī, *n.*   *cloth*

(33) Lesson Thirty-Three

A. FOURTH DECLENSION NEUTER NOUNS

Fourth declension neuter is a cousin of the fourth declension. Study the paradigms below and notice how the fourth declension neuter differs from regular fourth declension.

FOURTH DECLENSION NEUTER

ū	ua
ūs	uum
ū	ibus
ū	ua
ū	ibus

FOURTH DECLENSION

us	ūs
ūs	uum
uī	ibus
um	ūs
ū	ibus

There are very few fourth declension neuter nouns. Decline the two fourth neuter nouns from List 12.

B. NOUN-ADJECTIVE PHRASES

Translate the noun-adjective phrases below into Latin in all five cases. Remember to make the adjective agree with the noun it describes in gender, number, and case.

1. a sharp horn

Nominative   *cornu acutum*

Genitive   *cornūs acutī*

Dative   _____

Accusative   _____

Ablative   _____

2. small knees

Nominative   _____

Genitive   _____

Dative   _____

Accusative   _____

Ablative   _____

3. many horns

Nominative   _____

Genitive   _____

Dative   _____

Accusative   _____

Ablative   _____

4. a red knee

Nominative   _____

Genitive   _____

Dative   _____

Accusative   _____

Ablative   _____

C. TRANSLATION

Translate the sentences below.

1. Vetula Claudiam et Iūliam docēbat et nēnt et texunt. _____

_____

2. Haec vetula erat avia Claudiae. _____

_____

3. Vetula multam artem habuit quod multum ūsum habūerat. _____

_____

4. Lānam nēbat et textum texēbat cum celeritāte. _____

_____

5. Haec līnea colōrēs multōs habuit. _____

6. Hi colōrēs erant caeruleus, ruber, flāvus, et viridis. _____

_____

7. Iūlius, Claudius, et Saxum hīs cornibus canēbant et simulābant esse mīlitēs. _____

_____

_____

8. Puerī currēbant stulte. _____

9. Tela huius vetulae cecidit et avia Claudiae offensam multam habuit! _____

_____

10. "Mea culpa," clāmāvērunt Claudius, Iūlius, et Saxum. _____

_____

D. TIDBIT

Did you know that the Latin name for Jesus, *Iesus,* is a fourth declension noun?

34 Lesson Thirty-Four

A. DEMONSTRATIVE ADJECTIVE ILLE, ILLA, ILLUD

Below is another demonstrative adjective, the *ille, illa, illud* chant. In contrast to the *hic* chant, this chant means *that*, referring to a noun which is farther from the speaker. In the plural, it means *those*. Review Lesson 32 and compare the demonstrative adjectives *hic* and *ille*.

Study the paradigm of *ille, illa, illud* below.

SINGULAR (THAT)

CASE	MASCULINE	FEMININE	NEUTER
Nominative	ille	illa	illud
Genitive	illīus	illīus	illīus
Dative	illī	illī	illī
Accusative	illum	illam	illud
Ablative	illō	illā	illō

PLURAL (THOSE)

CASE	MASCULINE	FEMININE	NEUTER
Nominative	illī	illae	illa
Genitive	illōrum	illārum	illōrum
Dative	illīs	illīs	illīs
Accusative	illōs	illās	illa
Ablative	illīs	illīs	illis

Consider these nominative singular examples:

<u>Masculine</u>   <u>Feminine</u>   <u>Neuter</u>

ille puer — *that boy*   illa puella — *that girl*   illud saxum — *that rock*

Now look at a sentence which uses these phrases in different cases:

(Nom.) (Dat.)   (Acc.)   (V-t)

Ille puer illae puellae illud saxum dat.   *That boy gives that girl that rock.*

Now look over these same examples in the nominative plural.

<u>Masculine</u>   <u>Feminine</u>   <u>Neuter</u>

illī puerī — *those boys*   illae puellae — *those girls*   illa saxa — *those rocks*

(Nom.)   (Dat.)   (Acc.)(V.)

Illī puerī illīs puellīs illa saxa dant.   *Those boys give those girls those rocks.*

B. NOUN-ADJECTIVE PHRASES

Translate the noun-adjective phrases below according to the formulas given. One is done as an example.

1. accusative singular: this color   *hunc colōrem*

                      that color   *illum colōrem*

2. dative singular: this old woman   _____

                      that old woman   _____

3. nominative plural: these plans   _____

                      those plans   _____

4. genitive singular: this spider   _____

                      that spider   _____

5. ablative plural: these downfalls   _____

                      those downfalls   _____

C. TRANSLATION

Translate the sentences below into Latin.

1. Julius was watching that spider. _____

_____

2. That spider was spinning this web near that building.

_____

_____

3. Those insects were trapped by that spider._____

_____

4. That spider's web was those insects' downfall! _____

_____

D. SYNOPSIS

Do a synopsis of the verb *mutō, mutāre, mutāvī, mutātum* in the third person singular.

TENSE	SYNOPSIS	TRANSLATION
present		
imperfect		
future		
perfect		
pluperfect		
future perfect		

Now do a synopsis of the verb above in the passive voice, third person singular.

TENSE	SYNOPSIS	TRANSLATION
present		
imperfect		
future		

E. DERIVATIVE DIGGING

Choose one of the derivatives from the following list. Look up the definition of your derivative and write its meaning. Then use the derivative in an interesting sentence.

Derivatives: superb, simulate, immutable, offense.

Definition: _____

_____

Sentence: _____

_____

(35) Lesson Thirty-Five

A. ABLATIVE OF ACCOMPANIMENT

When someone is in company with someone else, the ablative case is used with the preposition *cum*, meaning *with, along with, or in company with.* Study the examples below.

> *Saxum lānam cum Iūliā net.*   Saxum is spinning wool with Julia.

> *Claudius in lūdō cum Iūliō contendet.*   Claudius will compete with Julius in the game.

N.B. Several uses of the ablative case can be translated into English by using the preposition *with.*

Notice the differences in the ablatives below.

> Ablative of Accompaniment: (Who is Julia with?)

> > *Iūlia textum cum Claudiā tēxit.*   Julia weaves the cloth with Claudia.

> Ablative of Means: (What does Julia weave with?)

> > *Iūlia textum tēlā tēxit.*   Julia weaves the cloth with a loom.

Remember that the ablative of means does not use a preposition in Latin.

> Ablative of Manner: (How does Julia weave?)

> > *Iūlia textum cum celeritāte tēxit.*   Julia weaves the cloth with speed.

B. TRANSLATION: LATIN TO ENGLISH

Translate the sentences below. Identify the ablative used in each one. Choose from means, manner, time when, time during, place where, place from which, personal agent, accompaniment.

Some sentences contain more than one use of the ablative case.

1. Iūlius et Claudius gladiīs simulābant pugnāre. _____

_____

Ablative of *gladiīs*? _____

2. Iūlius cum Claudiō pugnābat tertiā horā. _____

_____

Ablative of *cum Claudiō*? _____

Ablative of *tertiā hōra*? _____

3. Claudius cum arte pugnābat. _____

_____

Ablative of *cum arte*? _____

4. Iūlia, Saxum, et Claudia ab lītore ad Iūlium et Claudium ambulāverant. _____

_____

_____

Ablative of *ab lītore*? _____

C. ABLATIVE OF ACCOMPANIMENT COMPOSITION

Write your own Latin sentence which includes the ablative of accompaniment. Provide the translation of your sentence.

Sentence: _____

_____

Translation: _____

_____

D. TRANSLATION: ENGLISH TO LATIN

Translate the sentences below into Latin. Be sure to make the demonstrative adjectives match the nouns they describe in *gender, number, and case.*

1. Julia is this maiden. _____

2. Claudia pretended to be that goddess. _____

_____

3. That boy throws Saxum this ball. _____

4. Those plans will be changed. _____

5. These old women have watched that king's departure from that island. _____

_____

6. Those horns will announce this arrival. _____

_____

36 Lesson Thirty-Six
The Story of Arachne

Translate the story of Arachne.

1. Minerva erat dea sapientiae. _____

_____

2. Minerva quoque artēs nentis et texentis regēbat. _____

_____

3. Arachnē erat virgō perīta in nente et texente. _____

_____

4. Habuit ūsum multum acū. _____

_____

5. Arachnē lānam nēvit et textum tēxit pulchrē sed erat superba. ____

_____

6. Virgō stulta Minervam prōvocāvit contendere in texente. _____

_____

7. Minerva offensam multam dēmōnstrāvit. _____

_____

8. Simulāvit esse vetula et Arachnē cōnsilium dedit, "Nē audē deam prōvocāre." _____

_____

_____

9. Sed Arachnē vetulae, "Minervam," inquit, "nōn timeō." _____

_____

10. Tum Minerva apparuit et dīxit, "Contendam tēcum." _____

_____

11. Minerva et Arachnē ad tēlās sedēbant et colōrēs rubrī, caeruleae, et viridis texēbant. _____

_____

_____

12. Minerva Iōvem et deōs aliōs fabricāvit. _____

_____

13. In fābulis aliīs, Minerva offensam deōrum dēmōnstrāvit quod virī et fēminae audēbant cum deīs

contendere. _____

_____

_____

14. Arachnē picturās peccatōrum deōrum dēmōnstrāvit. _____

_____

15. Minerva erat īrāta ad Arachnen* et textum virginis divellit. _____

_____

16. Dea frontem Arachnēs tetigit et Arachne peccātum sua vīdit. _____

_____

17. Tum Arachnē temptāvit sē necāre. _____

_____

18. Sed Minerva misercordiam habuit et Arachnē mutāvit. _____

_____

19. Arachnē erat arānea. _____

20. Iam Arachnē līneam net et tēlās tēxit et bēstiolās inlaqueāt. _____

GLOSSARY

1. ad *(prep. with acc.)* at, to, toward
2. alius, -a, -um other
3. appāreō, -ēre, *apparuī, apparitum* appear
4. Arachnen *Greek accusative form of Arachne*
5. Arachnēs *Greek genetive form of Arachne*
6. dēmōnstrō, -āre, *-āvī, -ātum* show
7. dico, -ere, *dīxī, dictum* tell, say
8. divello, -ere, *-vellī, -velsum* tear apart
9. frons, frontis, *f.* forehead
10. iam (adv.) now
11. iratus, -a, -um angry
12. necō, -āre, *-āvī, -ātum* kill
13. nentis (gen.) of spinning
    nente (abl.) spinning
14. quoque also
15. se himself, herself, itself
16. superbus, -a, -um proud
17. suus, -a, -um your
18. tecum with you
19. temptō, -āre, *-āvī, -ātum* try
20. texentis (gen.) of weaving
    texente (abl.) weaving
21. tectum, -ī weaving, cloth
22. timeō, -ēre, *timuī, -__* fear
23. tum (adv.) then
24. vetula, -ae, *f.* old woman

Unit Six Review

A. PRINCIPAL PARTS REVIEW

Give the four principal parts for the verbs below:

VERB	1ST PART	2ND PART	3RD PART	4TH PART
1. weave	_____	_____	_____	_____
2. spin	_____	_____	_____	_____
3. change	_____	_____	_____	_____

B. VERB SYNOPSIS REVIEW

Do a verb synopsis for *contendō, contendere, contendī, contentum* in the first person plural, active voice.

Tense	Synopsis	Translation
present		
imperfect		
future		
perfect		
pluperfect		
future perfect		

Now do a verb synopsis for *prōvocō, -āre, -āvī, -ātum* in the first person plural, passive voice.

Tense	Synopsis	Translation
present		
imperfect		
future		

C. FOURTH DECLENSION REVIEW

Decline the Fourth Declension and Fourth Declension Neuter nouns below.

FOURTH DECLENSION

Case	Singular	Plural
Nominative	adventus	
Genitive	adventūs	
Dative		
Accusative		
Ablative		

FOURTH DECLENSION NEUTER

Case	Singular	Plural
Nominative	cornū	
Genitive	cornūs	
Dative		
Accusative		
Ablative		

D. DEMONSTRATIVE ADJECTIVE REVIEW

Decline the demonstrative adjectives *hic* and *ille* from memory. Then check any errors in red.

HIC CHANT

(singular, meaning *this***)**

Masculine	Feminine	Neuter
hic		

(plural, meaning *these***)**

Masculine	Feminine	Neuter
hī		

ILLE CHANT

(singular, meaning *that*)

Masculine	Feminine	Neuter
ille		

(plural, meaning *those*)

Masculine	Feminine	Neuter
illī		

E. ABLATIVE REVIEW

Translate and identify the correct use of the ablative for each of the sentences below. Possible ablatives are *means, manner, time when, time during, place where, place from which, personal agent, accompaniment*

1. Iūlia ambulat tertiā hōrā. _____

   Ablative of _____

2. Iūlia ambulat cum celeritāte. _____

   Ablative of _____

3. Iūlia ambulat cum Saxō. _____

   Ablative of _____

4. Iūlia ambulat ab aedificiō. _____

   _____

   Ablative of _____

5. Iūlia ambulat in aedificiō. _____

   _____

   Ablative of _____

6. Iūlia textum texēbat tēlā. _____

_____

Ablative of _____

7. Textum texēbātur ab Iūliā. _____

Ablative of _____

F. TRANSLATION

Translate the sentences below.

1. Manus virginis acum acūtam habuit cum arte._____

_____

2. Arachnē sapientiam Minervae nōn auscultāverat. _____

_____

3. Vetulae cum virginibus exitum mīlitum spectābunt. _____

_____

4. Claudia Iūliae textum caeruleum texūerat tēlā._____

_____

5. Dea nēbat cum arte quod habuit ūsum multum. _____

_____

G. DERIVATIVE REVIEW

Give the Latin origin for the English derivatives below. Also give the definition for each derivative, using an English dictionary if necessary.

DERIVATIVE	LATIN ORIGIN	DEFINITION
1. sapient	_____	_____
2. manumit	_____	_____
3. audacious	_____	_____
4. celerity	_____	_____
5. immutable	_____	_____

Unit 7

13 List Thirteen

VOCABULARY

Memorize the following Latin words and their translations.

WORD	DERIVATIVE	TRANSLATION
1. nauta, -ae, *m.*	_____	*sailor**
2. nāvis, nāvis, *f.*	_____	*ship*
3. rēmus, -ī, *m.*	_____	*oar*
4. fluctus, -ūs, *m.*	_____	*wave (of the sea)*
5. portus, -ūs, *m.*	_____	*harbor*
6. mīles, mīlitis, *m.*	_____	*soldier*
7. exercitus, -ūs, *m.*	_____	*army*
8. rēgnum, -ī, *n.*	_____	*kingdom*
9. impetus, -ūs, *m.*	_____	*an attack*
10. navigō, -āre, -āvi, -ātum	_____	*sail*
11. remigō, -āre, -āvī, -ātum	_____	*row*

* *Nauta* is a masculine noun even though it is from the first declension. It is sometimes called a "PAIN" word because it is masculine when you would expect it to be feminine. Other "PAIN" words include

     P — pīrāta (pirate), poēta (poet)
     A — agricola (farmer)
     I — incola (settler — can be masculine or feminine)
     N — nauta (sailor)

12. oppugnō, -āre, -āvī, -ātum   _____   *attack*

13. veniō, -īre, vēnī, ventum   _____   *come*

14. inveniō, -īre, -vēnī, -ventum   _____   *find, come upon*

15. conveniō, -īre, -vēnī, -ventum   _____   *assemble*

16. perveniō, -īre, -vēnī, -ventum   _____   *arrive, reach***

17. audiō, -īre, -īvī, -ītum   _____   *hear*

18. dormiō, -īre, -īvī, -ītum   _____   *sleep*

19. impediō, -īre, -īvī, -ītum   _____   *hinder*

20. muniō, -īre, -īvī, -ītum   _____   *fortify, build*

REVIEW WORDS

1. audācia, -ae, *f.*   *boldness*
2. cadō, -ere, cecidi, cāsum   *fall*
3. cūra, -ae, *f.*   *care, worry*
4. fleō, -ēre, flēvī, flētum   *weep*
5. fugiō, -ere, fūgī, fugitum   *flee from*
6. īnsula, -ae, *f.*   *island*
7. lītus, lītōris, *n.*   *seashore*
8. lūgeō, lūgēre, lūxī, -----   *grieve, mourn*
9. manus, -ūs, *f.*   *hand, band of men*
10. mare, maris, *n.*   *sea*
11. perīculōsus, -a, -um   *dangerous*
12. regō, -ere, rēxī, rēctum   *rule*
13. simulō, -āre, -āvī, -ātum   *pretend*

** *Perveniō* requires the preposition *ad* (translated as *at* here) because it implies motion from one place to another. For example:

    Iūlius pervenit ad portum.   *Julius arrives at the harbor.*

    Remember that *ad* takes the accusative case.

(37) Lesson Thirty-Seven

A. FOURTH CONJUGATION VERBS

Fourth Conjugation is made up of verbs whose present stem ends in *-i* and it is the last verb conjugation you will be learning. The present stem of fourth conjugation verbs is found by removing the *-ō* from the first principal part of the verb. The present stem also acts as a singular command. To form a plural command *-te* is added to the present stem. The second principal part of fourth conjugation verbs ends in *-īre*. Fourth conjugation verbs act like third conjugation i-stems. *Audiō* (hear) will be used to represent the fourth conjugation (active voice) in the paradigm below:

Four principal parts: *audiō, audīre, audīvī, audītum*
Present stem: *audi-*
Singular command: Audī. *Hear or Listen to.*
Plural command: Audīte. *Hear or Listen to.*

Notice that the present tense endings are the same as for first and second conjugation verbs. Highlight the present tense endings *-ō, -s, -t, -mus, -tis, -nt* in the present tense paradigm below.

PRESENT

audiō — *I hear*	audīmus — *we hear*
audīs — *you hear*	audītis — *you (pl.) hear*
audit — *he, she, it hears*	audiunt — *they hear*

The imperfect tense behaves like third conjugation verbs. Highlight the imperfect endings *-ēbam, -ēbās, -ebāt, -ēbāmus, -ēbātis, -ēbant.*

IMPERFECT

audiēbam — *I was hearing*	audiēbāmus — *we were hearing*
audiēbās — *you were hearing*	audiēbātis — *you (pl.) were hearing*
audiēbat — *he, she, it was hearing*	audiēbant — *they were hearing*

The future tense also behaves like the third conjugation. Highlight the future tense endings *-am, -ēs, -et, -ēmus, -ētis, -ent.*

FUTURE

audiam — *I will hear*	audiēmus — *we will hear*
audiēs — *you will hear*	audiētis — *you (pl.) will hear*
audiet — *he, she, it will hear*	audient — *they will hear*

The perfect, pluperfect, and future perfect all add endings to the perfect stem, which is formed from the third principal part in the same way as other conjugations.

Write the **perfect stem** for *audiō, audīre, audīvī, audītum* on the line.

Perfect stem:_____

PERFECT

audīvī — *I heard*	audīvimus — *we heard*
audīvistī — *you heard*	audīvistis — *you (pl.) heard*
audīvit — *he, she, it heard*	audīvērunt — *they heard*

PLUPERFECT

audīveram — *I had heard*	audīverāmus — *we had heard*
audīverās — *you had heard*	audīverātis — *you (pl.) had heard*
audīverat — *he, she, it had heard*	audīverant — *they had heard*

FUTURE PERFECT

audīverō — *I will have heard*	audīverimus — *we will have heard*
audīveris — *you will have heard*	audīveritis — *you (pl.) will have heard*
audīverit — *he, she, it, will have heard*	audīverint — *they will have heard*

B. FOURTH CONJUGATION STEMS

Give the present and perfect stems for the fourth conjugation verbs below.

VERB	PRESENT STEM	PERFECT STEM
1. muniō	_____	_____
2. veniō	_____	_____
3. impediō	_____	_____
4. dormiō	_____	_____

C. FOURTH CONJUGATION PRACTICE

Translate the fourth conjugation verbs below and identify the tense of each one.

VERB	TRANSLATION	TENSE
1. audit	_____	_____
2. audīvit	_____	_____
3. veniēbat	_____	_____
4. vēnerat	_____	_____
5. dormiēmus	_____	_____
6. dormīverimus	_____	_____
7. munītis	_____	_____
8. munīvistis	_____	_____
9. muniētis	_____	_____

D. VERB CONJUGATIONS

Translate the verbs below into Latin. Identify the conjugation of each verb (1st, 2nd, 3rd, 3rd -stem, or 4th).

VERB	TRANSLATION	CONJUGATION
1. You (sing) were sailing.	_____	_____
2. We will find.	_____	_____
3. They had slept.	_____	_____
4. You (plur.) are falling.	_____	_____
5. She did flee.	_____	_____
6. I will mourn.	_____	_____

E. DERIVATIVE DIGGING

Look up the English word *impede* and write its definition on the lines below. What is its Latin origin?

Definition of *impede*: _____

_____

Latin origin: _____

Use the word *impede* in a sentence. _____

_____

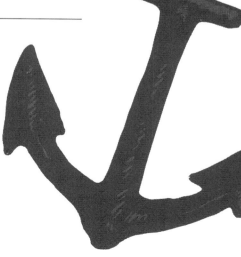

242 Lesson Thirty-Seven

(38) Lesson Thirty-Eight

A. MORE PRACTICE WITH 4TH CONJUGATION

Fill in the verb synopses below. The formula is *third person singular* and you will do a verb from each of the four conjugations.

FIRST CONJUGATION: navigō, navigāre, navigāvī, navigātum

Tense	Synopsis	Translation
present		
imperfect		
future		
perfect		
pluperfect		
future perfect		

SECOND CONJUGATION: fleō, flēre, flēvī, flētum

Tense	Synopsis	Translation
present		
imperfect		
future		
perfect		
pluperfect		
future perfect		

THIRD CONJUGATION: regō, regere, rēxī, rēctum

Tense	Synopsis	Translation
present		
imperfect		
future		
perfect		
pluperfect		
future perfect		

FOURTH CONJUGATION: veniō, venīre, vēnī, ventum

Tense	Synopsis	Translation
present		
imperfect		
future		
perfect		
pluperfect		
future perfect		

B. TRANSLATION

Translate the sentences below. Underline fourth conjugation verbs.

1. Līberī et Saxum sunt nautae perītī. _____

_____

_____

2. Iūlia et Claudia nāviculam* in portū navigābant, sed puerī et Saxum nāviculam remigābant rēmīs.

_____

_____

3. Magnī et multī** fluctūs naviculās impedīvērunt. _____

_____

4. Magnus fluctus nāviculam puerōrum oppugnāvit, et Saxum in portum cecidit! _____

_____

5. "Ubi est Saxum?" Claudius vocāvit. _____

_____

6. Puellae Claudium audīvērunt et Saxum in marī citō invēnērunt. _____

_____

7. Līberī et Saxum ad lītus pervēnērunt. _____

_____

C. ETYMOLOGY

Write an etymology for the English derivative *reign*:

_____

_____

* A *nāvicula* is a small ship. Translate it as *boat*.
** The adjective *multus* is sometimes connected to another adjective by the conjunction *et*. In English we would not usually translate *et*. For example, the phrase *multae et pulchrae feminae* can simply be translated *many beautiful women*.

14 List Fourteen

VOCABULARY

Memorize the following Latin words and their translations. Learn the principal parts of the verbs and the genitive and gender of nouns.

WORD	DERIVATIVE	TRANSLATION
1. ariēs, ariētis, *m.*	_____	*ram*
2. vellus, velleris, *n.*	_____	*fleece*
3. meridiēs, -ēī, *m.*	_____	*noon*
4. speciēs, -eī, *f.*	_____	*appearance*
5. rēs, reī, *f.*	_____	*thing, affair, matter*
6. aciēs, acieī, *f.*	_____	*line of battle, straight line*
7. fidēs, fideī, *f.*	_____	*faith*
8. nuntius, -ī, *m.*	_____	*messenger*
9. dracō, dracōnis, *m.*	_____	*dragon*
10. dens, dentis, *m.*	_____	*tooth*
11. ancora, -ae, *f.*	_____	*anchor*
12. corōna, -ae, *f.*	_____	*crown*
13. hērōs, hērōis, *m.*	_____	*hero*

*   *This word does not appear in the genitive and dative plural*

14. patruus, -ī, *m.* _____ *uncle (father's brother)*

15. iugum, -ī, *n.* _____ *a yoke*

16. adulēscēns, adulēscentis, *m.* _____ *young man*

17. nāvicula, -ae, *f.* _____ *small boat*

18. pōtiō, potiōnis, *f.* _____ *potion*

19. dēfendō, -ere, dēfendī, dēfēnsum _____ *defend*

20. līberō, -āre, -āvī, -ātum _____ *set free, liberate*

REVIEW WORDS

1. aedificō, -āre, -āvī, -ātum — *build*
2. arō, -āre, -āvī, -ātum — *plow*
3. aureus, -a, -um — *golden*
4. avunculus, -ī, *m.* — *uncle (mother's brother)*
5. columba, -ae, *f.* — *dove*
6. cōnsilium, -ī, *n.* — *plan, advice*
7. diēs, -eī, *m.* — *day*
8. flamma, -ae, *f.* — *flame*
9. Graecia, -ae, *f.* — *Greece*
10. ignis, ignis, *m.* — *fire*
11. īnsula, -ae, *f.* — *island*
12. lāna, -ae, *f.* — *wool*
13. lūcus, -ī, *m.* — *grove*
14. manus, -ūs, *f.* — *band of men (also hand)*
15. nuntiō, -āre, -āvī, -ātum — *announce*
16. oppugnō, -āre, -āvī, -ātum — *attack*
17. rēx, rēgis, *m.* — *king*
18. spēs, -eī, *f.* — *hope*
19. taurus, -ī, *m.* — *bull*
20. vigilō, -āre, -āvī, -ātum — *guard*

(39) Lesson Thirty-Nine

A. FIFTH DECLENSION NOUNS

Fifth Declension is the last Latin noun family. This small declension consists of mostly feminine nouns. Study the 5th declension endings and then highlight those endings on the word *res*.

5th DECLENSION

ēs	ēs
ēī	ērum
ēī	ēbus
em	ēs
ē	ēbus

rēs	rēs
rēī	rērum
rēī	rēbus
rem	rēs
rē	rēbus

B. DECLENSION IDENTIFICATION

Identify the declensions of the nouns below by looking at the genitive singular forms of the nouns below.

NOMINATIVE	GENITIVE	DECLENSION
1. ariēs	_____	_____
2. meridiīs	_____	_____
3. vellus	_____	_____

4. dracō   _____   _____

5. corōna   _____   _____

6. lūcus   _____   _____

7. fidēs   _____   _____

8. iugum   _____   _____

C. CONJUGATION IDENTIFICATION

Identify the conjugation of the verbs below by paying attention to the first two principal parts

VERB	CONJUGATION
1. audeō, audēre	_____
2. veniō, venīre	_____
3. remigō, remigāre	_____
4. faciō, facere	_____
5. cadō, cadere	_____

D. TRANSLATION: ENGLISH TO LATIN

The appearance of the line of battle at noon gave hope to the army.

_____

_____

40 Lesson Forty

A. PERSONAL PRONOUNS & POSSESSIVE ADJECTIVES FOR FIRST & SECOND PERSON

Personal pronouns for first and second person are represented by the *ego* and *tū* chants. They are used for emphasis. Study the personal pronoun chants and meanings below.

FIRST PERSON

Case	Singular	Plural
Nominative	ego — *I* (subject)	nōs — *we* (subject)
Genitive	meī — *of me*	nostrum — *of us*
Dative	mihi — *to me* (indirect object)	nōbīs — *to us* (indirect object)
Accusative	mē — *me* (direct object or OP)	nōs — *us* (direct object or OP)
Ablative	mē — *me*	nōbīs — *us*

SECOND PERSON

Case	Singular	Plural
Nominative	tū — *you* (subject)	vōs — *you* (subject)
Genitive	tuī — *of you*	vestrum — *of you*
Dative	tibi — *to you* (indirect object)	vōbīs — *to you* (indirect object)
Accusative	tē — *you* (direct object or OP)	vōs — *you* (direct object or OP)
Ablative	tē — *you*	vōbis — *you*

Consider these examples containing personal pronouns:

Tū mihi vellus ariētis dedistī.	*You gave me the ram's fleece.*
Nuntius mē vigilābit.	*The messenger will guard me.*
Nōs vobīscum navigābāmus	*We were sailing with you (pl).*

N.B. The ablative of accompaniment attaches *cum* (with) on the end of the pronoun, forming one word:

mēcum (with me)   *nōbīscum* (with us)   *tēcum* (with you)   *vōbīscum* (with you)

Personal pronoun possessive adjectives:

Personal pronouns (such as *ego, tū, nōs,* and *vōs*) do not have a genitive case. To show possession, we use the adjectives listed below. Like other adjectives, these must match the nouns they describe in gender, number, and case.

Masculine	Feminine	Neuter	Translation
meus	mea	meum	*my*
noster	nostra	nostrum	*our*
tuus	tua	tuum	*your (singular)*
vester	vestra	vestrum	*your (plural)*

Consider these examples containing personal pronoun possessive adjectives:

Ancora mea est in nāviculā tuā.   *My anchor is in your boat.*

Fidēs nostra est spēs vestra.   *Our faith is your (pl.) hope.*

Hērōs noster adulēscentī meō corōnam tuam dat.   *Our hero gives my young man your crown.*

B. TRANSLATION

Translate sentences, commands, and questions containing fourth conjugation verbs, personal pronouns, and personal possessive adjectives.

1. Audī, Iūlī, cōnsilium meum._____

2. Veniēsne, Claudia, mēcum ad portum? _____

_____

3. Convenīte, mīlitēs, in aciē. _____

_____

4. Num nauta dracōnem oppugnāvit diē? _____

_____

5. Nonne hērōs vester fidem in Deō habet?_____

_____

C. TRANSLATION: LATIN TO ENGLISH

Translate sentences containing personal pronouns and forms of the adjectives *meus, noster, tuus,* and *vester.*

1. Ego tibi potiōnem tuam dedī._____

2. Mīlitēs vōs vigilābunt. _____

3. Nōs convēnerāmus in aciē. _____

_____

4. Nautae nostrī nāviculam tuam remigant. _____

_____

5. Tū mē nōn inveniēs._____

A. ABLATIVE OF SEPARATION

Separation **which does not involve physical movement away from some thing or person** is shown by the ablative case with the preposition *ā, ab,* or sometimes with no preposition. Usually, the preposition is used with persons and concrete nouns but omitted before abstract nouns (invisible qualities such as love, fear, anger, etc.). Consider the examples of the ablative of separation below.

    1. *Adulēscēns taurōs ab iugō liberāvit.*   *The young man freed the bulls from the yoke.*

Notice that the yoke is a concrete noun, a noun you can see and touch. Therefore, a preposition is used.

    2. *Deus adulēscēntem curā liberāvit.*   *God freed the young man from care/worry.*

Care or *worry* is an invisible noun, a quality. Therefore no preposition is used.

Do not confuse the *ablative of separation* with the *ablative of place from which:*

    3. *Adulēscēns ā taurīs ambulāvit.*   *The young man walked away from the bulls.*

In this example, the young man is physically moving away from something by *walking.*

B. ABLATIVE TRANSLATION

Translate the sentences below, and tell which ablative is being used.

1. Nautae portum ab impetū dēfendēbant. _____

_____

Ablative of _____

2. Mīlitēs in aciē conveniunt. _____

_____

Ablative of _____

3. Exercitūs ā regnō ambulāverint. _____

_____

Ablative of _____

4. Nāvem rēmis remigābimus. _____

Ablative of _____

C. PERSONAL PRONOUN TRANSLATION

Practice using personal pronouns and personal pronoun possessive adjectives as you translate these sentences into Latin. Pronouns and pronoun possessive adjectives are in bold type.

1. **I** had slept on **my** island. _____

2. **You** did not hear **our** rams. _____

3. **Your** sailors are building **us** little boats. _____

4. **We** will find **our** faith in God. _____

42 Lesson Forty-Two
Jason and the Golden Fleece

Translate the story of Jason and the Golden Fleece.

1. Aesōn erat rēx Thessaliae sed nōn cupīvit rēgem esse. _____

_____

2. Aesōn fratrī Peliae corōnam dedit donec Iāsōn, fīlius Aesonis, erat adulēscēns. _____

_____

_____

3. Sed patruus Iāsōnis adulēscēntī corōnam nōn cupīvit dāre. _____

_____

4. Pelias Iāsōnem mīsit Vellus Aureum invenīre. _____

_____

5. Iāsōn Argum rogāvit nāvem magnam aedificāre. _____

_____

6. Nōmen nāvis erat "Argō". _____

_____

7. Iasōn adulēscēntēs Graeciae invitāvit in nāve navigāre. _____

_____

8. Adulēscēntēs hēroēs erant et vocābantur Argonautās. _____

_____

9. Iāsōn et Argonautae ad regnum Colchidis navigāvērunt._____

_____

10. Rēx Colchidis Iāsōnem imperāvit: "Pone iugum in flammās spirantēs bovēs et sere dentēs dracōnis ."

_____

_____

_____

11. Mīlitēs ex dentibus vēnērunt et Iāsōnem oppugnāvērunt. _____

_____

12. Sed Medea, uxor Iāsōnis, iuvāvit arte magicā et Iāsōn mīlitēs superāvit. _____

_____

_____

13. Dracō Vellus Aureum vigilābat. _____

_____

14. Iāsōn dracōnī potiōnem dedit et dracō dormīvit._____

_____

15. Iāsōn Vellus Aureum cēpit et ad Thessaliam cum Argonautīs navigāvit. _____

_____

_____

GLOSSARY

1. aedificō, -āre, -āve, -ātum   *build*
2. Aesōn   *King of Thessaly*
3. Argonautae, -ārum, *m.*   *Argonauts, heros of Greece*
4. Argus, -ī, *m.*   *100 eyed guardian of Io*
5. ars magica, artis magicae, *f.*   *magic, magic arts*
6. aureus, -a, -um   *golden*
7. bōs, bovis, *m.*   *bull*
8. capiō, -ere, cēpī, captum   *seize, capture*
9. Colchis, Colchidis, *f.*   *country on Eastern shore of the Black Sea*
10. cupiō, -īre, -īvī, -ītum   *wish, want, desire*
11. donec (conj.)   *up to the time when, until*
12. esse   *to be*
13. flammās spirantēs bovēs   *fire-breathing bulls*
14. Iāsōn, -onis, *m.*   *son of Aeson*
15. imperō, -āre, -āvī, -atum   *order*
16. invitō, -āre, -āve, -ātum   *invite*
17. iuvō, -are, iūvī, iūtum   *help*
18. Medea   *wife of Jason*
19. mittō, -ere, mīsī, missum   *send*
20. Pelias, -ae, *m.*   *brother of Aeson*
21. ponō, -ere, posuī, positum   *put, place*
22. rēgnum, -ī, *n.*   *kingdom*
23. serō, -ere, sēvī, satum   *sow, plant*
24. spirantēs   *breathing*
25. superō, -āre, -āvī, -atum   *conquer*
26. Thessalia, -ae, *f.*   *Thessaly, region in northern Greece*
27. uxor, uxoris, *f.*   *wife*

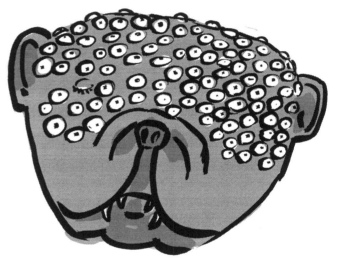

Unit Seven Review

A. FOURTH CONJUGATION REVIEW

Fill in the missing principal parts and meanings from memory. Compare your answers to List 13, then correct errors in red.

1st Part	2nd Part	3rd Part	4th Part	Meaning
veniō			ventum	
	convenīre			assemble
		audīvī		
impediō			impedītum	
	munīre			fortify, build
		dormīvī		
perveniō			perventum	
	invenīre			find, come upon

B. NOUN REVIEW

Give the genitive, gender, declension, and meaning for the nouns below from memory. Check your answers with Lists 13 and 14, correcting errors in red.

NOMINATIVE	GENITIVE	GENDER	DECLENSION	MEANING
1. nāvis				
2. fluctus				
3. rēs				
4. nauta				
5. regnum				

6. ariēs   _____   _____   _____   _____

7. fidēs   _____   _____   _____   _____

C. FOURTH CONJUGATION STEM REVIEW

Give the present and perfect stems for the fourth conjugation verbs below.

FOUR PRINCIPAL PARTS OF VERB	PRESENT STEM	PERFECT STEM
1. veniō, venīre, vēnī, ventum	_____	_____
2. audiō, audīre, audīvī, audītum	_____	_____

D. FOURTH CONJUGATION VERB REVIEW:

Translate the fourth conjugation verbs:

1. venīmus   _____

2. vēnimus   _____

3. veniēmus   _____

4. impedit   _____

5. impediet   _____

6. impedīvit   _____

7. munient   _____

8. muniunt   _____

9. munīverint   _____

10. convēnistis   _____

11. convenītis   _____

12. conveniēbātis   _____

E. SYNOPSES

Do a synopsis of the fourth conjugation verb *inveniō, invenīre, invēnī, inventum* in the second person singular.

Tense	Synopsis	Translation
present		
imperfect		
future		
perfect		
pluperfect		
future perfect		

Do a synopsis of the first conjugation verb *līberō, līberāre, līberāvi, līberātum* in the third person plural, passive voice.

Tense	Synopsis	Translation
present		
imperfect		
future		

F. FIFTH DECLENSION REVIEW

Decline the fifth declension noun *fidēs*.

fidēs	

Unit Seven Review

G. TRANSLATION

Translate the sentences below:

1. Nōs mīlitēs nostrōs conveniēmus in rēgnō tuō. _____

_____

2. Hērōs exercitum tuum ab impetū dracōnis dēfenderat. _____

_____

3. Ego nāviculam meam navigābō sed vōs nāvem vestram in portum remigābitis rēmis. _____

_____

_____

4. Speciēs mīlitum meridiē adulēscēntibus spem dedit. _____

_____

5. Tua fidēs tē līberat curā. _____

H. DERIVATIVES REVIEW

List five English derivatives from lists 13 and 14 and give their Latin origins.

DERIVATIVE	LATIN ORIGIN
1. _____	_____
2. _____	_____
3. _____	_____
4. _____	_____
5. _____	_____

Unit 8

15 Listt Fifteen

VOCABULARY

Memorize the following Latin words and their translations.

WORD	DERIVATIVE	TRANSLATION
1. ager, agrī , *m.*	_____	*field*
2. prātum, -ī , *n.*	_____	*meadow*
3. herba, -ae, *f.*	_____	*plant*
4. clīvus, -ī , *m.*	_____	*hill*
5. campus, -ī, *m.*	_____	*plain*
6. pōmum, -ī , *n.*	_____	*fruit*
7. ūva, -ae, *f.*	_____	*grape*
8. locus, -ī , *m.*	_____	*place*
9. līlium, -ī , *n.*	_____	*lily*
10. herbōsus, -a, -um	_____	*grassy*
11. purpureus, -a, -um	_____	*purple*
12. cārus, -a, -um	_____	*dear*
13. suus, -a, -um	_____	*his, her, its, their*
14. alius, -a, -ud	_____	*other, another*
15. delectō, -āre, -āvī, -ātum	_____	*delight*

16. errō, -āre, -āvī, -ātum   _____   *wander, be mistaken*

17. desiderō, -āre, -āvī, -ātum   _____   *miss, want*

18. floreō, -ēre, -uī, --------   _____   *flourish, bloom*

19. undique (adv.)   _____   *from all sides*

20. statim (adv.)   _____   *immediately*

REVIEW LIST

1. fleō, -ēre, -ēvī, -ētum   *weep*
2. vīnea, -ae, *f.*   *vineyard*
3. habitō, -āre, -āvī, -ātum   *live in, inhabit*
4. rōsa, -ae, *f.*   *rose*
5. albus, -a, -um   *white*
6. caeruleus, -a, -um   *blue*
7. flāvus, -a, -um   *yellow*
8. ruber, rubra, rubrum   *red*
9. silva, -ae, *f.*   *forest*
10. ubi   *where*
11. arō, -āre, -āvī, -ātum   *plow*
12. meus, mea, meum   *my*
13. tuus, tua, tuum   *your (singular)*
14. noster, nostra, nostrum   *our*
15. vester, vestra, vestrum   *your (plural)*
16. flōs, flōris, *m.*   *flower*
17. grāmen, grāminis, *n.*   *grass*
18. carpō, -ere, carpsī, carptum   *pluck*
19. edō, -ere, ēdī, ēsum   *eat*
20. dum   *while*
21. ōs, ōris, *n.*   *mouth*
22. propter (*prep. with acc.*)   *because of, on account of*
23. cupiō, cupere, cupīvī, cupītum   *wish, want, desire*
24. pōnō, ponere, posuī, positum   *put, place*

(43) Lesson Forty-Three

A. DEMONSTRATIVE ADJECTIVES *IS, EA, ID*

We have learned the demonstrative adjective chant *hic, haec, hoc* which means "this/these" and indicates nearness to the speaker. The demonstrative adjective *ille, illa, illud* means "that/those" and indicates greater distance from the speaker. But a third demonstrative adjective, *is, ea, id*, does not indicate a particular location. It simply shows that the noun it is describing has already been mentioned or is going to be explained.

Is, ea, id can mean "this/these" or "that/those." Like other demonstrative adjectives, *is, ea, id* comes **before** the noun it describes. Memorize the *is, ea, id* chant.

IS, EA, ID CHANT

(Singular)

Masculine	Feminine	Neuter
is	ea	id
eius	eius	eius
eī	eī	eī
eum	eam	id
eō	eā	eō

(Plural)

Masculine	Feminine	Neuter
eī	eae	ea
eōrum	eārum	eōrum
eīs	eīs	eīs
eōs	eās	ea
eīs	eīs	eīs

Consider these examples, comparing *is, ea, id* with *hic* and *ille*.

> Iūlia līlium carpsit. **Id** līlium album erat.
> *Julia plucked a lily. This (or that) lily was white.*

> Iūlia **hoc** līlium carpsit sed **illud** līlium non carpsit.
> *Julia plucked this lily but she did not pluck that lily.*

B. TRANSLATION: LATIN TO ENGLISH

Translate these sentences containing demonstrative adjectives.

1. Līberī et Saxum in hōc prātō errābant quod taurī magnī grāmen et herbās in illō prātō edēbant.

_____

_____

_____

_____

2. Flōrēs purpureī in eīs prātīs florēbant. _____

_____

3. Iūlia haec līlia alba carpsit dum Claudia illās rōsās rubrās carpsit. _____

_____

_____

4. Puellae magistrae eōs flōrēs dedērunt. _____

_____

5. Magistra delectābātur. _____

6. Puerī et Saxum uvās purpureās in prātō carpēbant et edēbant. _____

_____

7. Saxum ōs purpureum habuit propter eās uvās! _____

_____

8. Iūlius et Claudius magistrae uvās dedērunt. _____

_____

C. PASSIVE VERBS REVIEW

Practice translating these passive voice verbs.

1. delectābantur. _____

2. desiderāmur _____

3. oppugnāris _____

4. navigābitur _____

5. mutābor _____

Challenge: Add Latin subject nouns to go with the words above.

D. DERIVATIVE DIGGING

Try to use at least five derivatives from this list in a short paragraph. Underline the derivatives used.

_____

_____

_____

_____

_____

_____

_____

44 Lesson Forty-Four

A. PERSONAL PRONOUNS REVIEW

We learned the personal pronouns for first and second person in Lesson 40. Fill in the missing parts and translations.

FIRST PERSON

Case	Singular	Translation	Plural	Translation
Nominative	ego	I (SP)		
Genitive*	mei	of me	nostrum	
Dative				
Accusative				
Ablative				

SECOND PERSON

Case	Singular	Translation	Plural	Translation
Nominative	tū	you (SP)		
Genitive*	tuī	of you	vestrum	
Dative				
Accusative				
Ablative				

* Remember that possession is *not* shown by the genitive case. Instead, it is necessary to use the adjectives *meus, tuus, noster, and vester.*

B. PERSONAL PRONOUNS FOR THIRD PERSON

There is no personal pronoun for third person, *he, she, it, they*. Usually, the demonstrative pronoun *is, ea, id* is used. Until now, we have only used this chant as a demonstrative adjective meaning "this/ that" or "these/those." Consider what this chant means when it acts as a pronoun.

SINGULAR

CASE	Masculine	Feminine	Neuter
Nominative	is — *he* (SP)	ea — *she* (SP)	id — *it* (SP)
Genitive*	eius — *of him*	eius — *of her*	eius — *of it*
Dative	eī — *to him* (IO)	eī — *to her* (IO)	eī — *to it* (IO)
Accusative	eum — *him* (DO)	eam — *her* (DO)	id — *it* (DO)
Ablative	eō — *him*	eā — *her*	eō — *it*

PLURAL

CASE	Masculine	Feminine	Neuter
Nominative	eī — *they* (SP)	eae — *they* (SP)	ea — *they* (SP)
Genitive*	eōrum — *of them*	eārum — *of them*	eōrum — *of them*
Dative	eīs — *to them* (IO)	eīs — *to them* (IO)	eīs — *to them* (IO)
Accusative	eōs — *them* (DO)	eās — *them* (DO)	ea — *them* (DO)
Ablative	eīs — *them*	eīs — *them*	eīs — *them*

N.B. Because inanimate objects can be masculine or feminine, they can be translated as *it* instead of *he* or *she*.

*Again, the genitive is not used to show possession here.

C. POSSESSION IN THIRD PERSON

It is necessary to use the adjective *suus, sua, suum* to show possession in the third person. Like other adjectives, this one must also match the noun it describes in gender, number, and case.

Study the possessive adjective *suus*.

Masculine	Feminine	Neuter	Translation
suus	sua	suum	*his, her, its* (singular)
suus	sua	suum	*their* (plural)

N.B. You will need to use context clues to help you know if the intended meaning is singular or plural.

D. PERSONAL PRONOUN TRANSLATION

Practice translating *is, ea, id* as a pronoun (he, she, it, they) in the sentences below. The third person possessive adjective *suus, sua, suum* will also be used.

1. Iūlia līlia alba vīdit et Claudiae eā carpsit._____

_____

2. Iūlia Claudiae ea dedit et Claudia ab eīs delectābātur. _____

_____

3. Claudia sua līlia in aquā posuit et Claudiō ea dēmōnstrāvit. _____

_____

4. Ea Saxō unum līlium dedit. _____

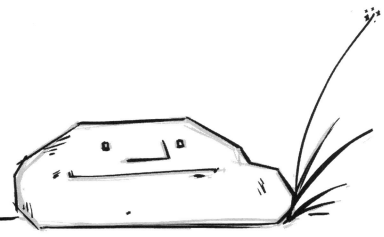

E. MORE PERSONAL PRONOUN TRANSLATION

Now translate these sentences which use *is, ea, id* as an adjective or a pronoun.

1. Saxum id līlium amāvit. _____

2. Iūlius uvās purpureās cūpīvit et is eās carpsit. _____

_____

3. Līberī eās ūvās edēbant. _____

4. Suī flōrēs in eō clīvō herbōsō florēbant. _____

_____

F. SYNOPSIS

Do a synopsis of the third conjugation verb *edō, edere, ēdī, ēsum* in the second person singular.

TENSE	SYNOPSIS	TRANSLATION
present		
imperfect		
future		
perfect		
pluperfect		
future perfect		

G. DERIVATIVE

Choose a derivative from List 15 and write its etymology.

Derivative: _____

Etymology: _____

_____

16 List Sixteen

A. VOCABULARY

Memorize the following Latin words and their translations.

WORD	DERIVATIVE	TRANSLATION
1. focus, -ī, *m.*	_____	*hearth, fireplace*
2. frūmentum, -ī, *n.*	_____	*grain (plural—crops)*
3. memoria, -ae, *f.*	_____	*memory*
4. capillus, -ī, *m.*	_____	*hair (often plural)*
5. palla, -ae, *f.*	_____	*cloak*
6. verbum, -ī, *n.*	_____	*word*
7. mittō, mittere, mīsī, missum	_____	*send*
8. incitō, -āre, -āvī, -ātum	_____	*urge*
9. raptō, -āre, -āvī, -ātum	_____	*snatch, seize*
10. adōrō, -āre, -āvī, -ātum	_____	*worship*
11. orō, -āre, -āvī, -ātum	_____	*beg, ask for*
12. grātus, -a, -um	_____	*grateful, pleasing*
13. cēterī, -ae, -a*	_____	*the rest (of)*
14. dīvīnus, -a, -um	_____	*divine*

* Usually plural. Singular form is *cēterus, -a, -um.*

15. vehementer (adv.) _____ *exceedingly, very much*

16. īrātus, -a, -um _____ *angry*

17. perterritus, -a, -um _____ *frightened*

18. subitō (adv.) _____ *suddenly*

19. et...et _____ *both...and*

20. nam (conj.) _____ *for*

REVIEW WORDS

1. caelum, -i, *n.*   *sky, heaven*
2. capiō, -ere, cēpī, captum   *capture*
3. carcer, carceris, *m.*   *prison*
4. coma, -ae, *f.*   *hair, leaves of a tree*
5. laborō, -āre, -āvī, -ātum   *work*
6. laudō, -āre, -āvī, -ātum   *praise*
7. lūna, -ae, *f.*   *moon*
8. mīlēs, mīlitis, *m.*   *soldier*
9. repente (adv.)   *suddenly*
10. spēs, speī, *f.*   *hope*
11. stella, -ae, *f.*   *star*
12. surgō, surgere, surrēxī, surrēctum   *rise up*
13. templum, -i, *n.*   *temple*

A. POSSESSIVE ADJECTIVES

Adjectives must match the nouns they describe in gender, number, and case. This includes the possessive adjectives *meus, tuus, suus, noster, and vester.*

Write the meaning of each possessive adjective below:

1. meus, -a, -um   _____

2. tuus, -a, -um   _____

3. suus, -a, -um (singular) _____

4. suus, -a, -um (plural)   _____

5. noster, nostra, nostrum   _____

6. vester, vestra, vestrum   _____

B. POSSESSIVE ADJECTIVE PHRASES

Translate the phrases below into Latin. Use the nominative case.

1. my memory   _____

2. your (plural) cloaks _____

3. our fireplace   _____

4. his word   _____

5. her word   _____

6. its word   _____

7. their word   _____

8. your (singular) place   _____

9. our plants   _____

10. his grapes   _____

C. MORE POSSESSIVE ADJECTIVE PHRASES

Now translate these same phrases using the accusative case.

1. my memory   _____

2. your (plural) cloaks   _____

3. our fireplace   _____

4. his word   _____

5. her word   _____

6. its word   _____

7. their word   _____

8. your (singular) place   _____

9. our plants   _____

10. his grapes   _____

D. REVIEW

Translate the sentences below into Latin using pronouns from the *is, ea, id* chant. Although these are pronouns they must still match the noun they represent in gender, number, and case.

Example:

Julia gave Claudia the fruit.
Iūlia Claudiae pōmum dedit.

Change to: Julia gave **her** the fruit.
Translation: Iūlia **eī** pōmum dedit.

1. Julia gave the fruit to Claudia.

      Iūlia Claudiae pōmum dedit.
      Change to: Julia gave **it** to Claudia.

      Translation: _____

2. Claudius is wandering on the hill.

      Claudius in clivō errat.
      Change to: **He** is wandering on the hill.

      Translation: _____

3. The children will walk on the plain.

      Līberī in campō ambulābunt.
      Change to: **They** will walk on **it**.

      Translation: _____

E. USE OF *ET...ET*

Study the sentence below and underline the word *et* :

> *Et Iūlia et Claudia Saxō pōmum dedērunt.*
> Both Julia and Claudia gave Saxum the fruit.

Translate these sentences containing *et...et*:

1. Et Claudius et Iūlius in clivō errābant. _____

_____

2. Et līberī et Saxum in campō ambulābunt. _____

_____

F. DERIVATIVE DIGGING

Choose one of the following derivatives, give its Latin origin, and look it up in a dictionary. Write the definition on the lines below. Then use your derivative correctly in an interesting sentence.

Derivative Choices: *capillary, raptor, missile, focal, vehement*

Derivative: _____

Latin origin: _____

Definition: _____

_____

Use the word in a sentence. _____

_____

46 Lesson Forty-Six

A. RELATIVE PRONOUNS

Study the relative pronoun chant and its meanings below.

SINGULAR

CASE	Masculine	Feminine	Neuter
Nominative	quī — *who, which*	quae — *who, which*	quod — *which*
Genitive	cuius — *whose, of whom, of which*	cuius — *whose, of whom, of which*	cuius — *of which*
Dative	cui — *to whom, to which*	cui — *to whom, to which*	cui — *to which*
Accusative	quem — *whom, which*	quam — *whom, which*	quod — *which*
Ablative	quō — *from, by, with whom, which*	quā — *from, by, with whom, which*	quō — *in, on, at, from, by, with which*

PLURAL

CASE	Masculine	Feminine	Neuter
Nominative	quī — *who, which*	quae — *who, which*	quae — *which*
Genitive	quōrum — *whose, of whom, of which*	quārum — *whose, of whom, of which*	quōrum — *of which*
Dative	quibus — *to whom, to which*	quibus — *to whom, to which*	quibus — *to which*
Accusative	quōs — *whom, which*	quās — *whom, which*	quae — *which*
Ablative	quibus — *from, by, with whom, which*	quibus — *from, by, with whom, which*	quibus — *in, on, at, from, by, with which*

A relative pronoun means *who* or *which* and relates to a noun which has already been mentioned in a sentence. The relative pronoun must agree with its *antecedent*, the noun to which it refers, in gender and number. The relative pronoun case, however, depends upon how it is used in its own clause.

Antecedent comes from two Latin words. *Ante* means "before" and *cedō* can mean "happen". Literally, the antecedent noun happens before the relative pronoun in a sentence. In the examples below parentheses will be placed around the clauses containing relative pronouns.

For example,

> The *young woman* (*who* gave Julia a rose) was wandering in a field.

In this example, we have the main sentence, "The young woman was wandering in a field." Inside the sentence is a relative clause, "who gave Julia a rose." The relative pronoun *who* refers to the young woman. *Who* in this example is the subject of its clause.

Now look at this example in Latin:

> *Virgō* (*quae* Iūliae rōsam dedit) in agrō errābat.

The antecedent noun *virgō* is feminine and singular so the form of the relative pronoun must also be feminine and singular. Because *who* in the example above is the subject of its own clause, it must also be nominative. *Quae* is feminine, singular, and nominative.

Study this new example:

> The *young woman* (*to whom* Julia gave a rose) was wandering in a field.

The *young woman* is the subject noun so the relative pronoun will still be feminine and singular. But this time the relative pronoun *to whom* must be translated into Latin in the dative case.

Study the Latin version of this sentence:

> *Virgō* (*cui* Iūlia rōsam dedit) in agrō errābat.

N.B. When translating the ablative of accompaniment the preposition *cum* is typically attached to the relative pronoun and translated as *with whom* or *with which*. For instance, quōcum, quācum, and quibuscum all mean *with whom*.

B. RELATIVE PRONOUN TRANSLATION

Try translating some other variations of this sentence which use the relative pronoun in different ways.

1. Virgō (quācum Iūlia errābat) rōsās carpit. _____

_____

2. Virgō (cuius rōsās Iūlia habet) aliās rōsās carpit. _____

_____

3. Rōsae (quas virgō carpsit) eam delectāvit. _____

_____

C. RELATIVE PRONOUN TRANSLATION

Translate these sentences containing relative pronouns into Latin.

1. The soldiers (to whom the women give grain) are grateful. _____

_____

2. The grapes (which delight Claudius) are purple. _____

_____

3. The lilies (which Julia wants) are flourishing in the grassy meadow. _____

_____

Challenge: Agricola (cuius ager iacet in campō) agrum arabāt. _____

_____

47 Lesson Forty-Seven

A. MORE PRACTICE WITH DEMONSTRATIVE ADJECTIVES

Translate the sentences below containing the demonstrative *is, ea, id* as an adjective.

1. Is puer in eō prātō errāverat. _____

_____

2. Iūlia et Claudia eōs flōrēs carpent in eō clīvō. _____

_____

3. These farmers were plowing this field from all sides. _____

_____

B. DEMONSTRATIVE PRONOUN TRANSLATION

Translate these sentences containing the demonstrative *is, ea, id* as a pronoun. These sentences refer to the sentences in section A.

1. Is in eō errāverat. _____

2. Iūlia et Claudia eōs carpent in eō. _____

_____

3. They (give pronoun) were plowing it from all sides. _____

_____

C. POSSESSIVE ADJECTIVE TRANSLATION

Translate sentences containing the possessive adjective *suus, sua, suum*

1. Is puer in suō prātō errāverat. _____

_____

2. Iūlia et Claudia suōs flōrēs carpent in suō clīvō. _____

_____

3. His farmers were plowing their fields from all sides. _____

_____

D. RELATIVE PRONOUN TRANSLATION

Translate sentences containing the relative pronoun *qui, quae, quod.*

1. Is puer (quī in suō prātō errāverat) clīvum scandit. _____

_____

2. Flōrēs (quos Iūlia et Claudia carpent) sunt pulchrī. _____

_____

3. The farmers (whose fields were being plowed) were working from all sides. _____

_____

E. ABLATIVE REVIEW

List the nine uses of the ablative case.

1. Ablative of _____

2. Ablative of _____

3. Ablative of _____

4. Ablative of _____

5. Ablative of _____

6. Ablative of _____

7. Ablative of _____

8. Ablative of _____

9. Ablative of _____

Translate the sentences and identify which ablatives are being used. Ablatives in the sentences are *italicized*.

1. Iūlius dracōnem *gladiō* pugnāvit. _____

_____

Ablative of _____

2. Puella *quācum* Iūlia ambulat est Claudia. _____

_____

Ablative of _____

3. Līberī *in campō* errābant. _____

_____

Ablative of _____

4. Deum adorāmus *cum spē.* _____

_____

Ablative of _____

5. Iūlius *ā carcere* vīrōs līberābat. _____

_____

Ablative of _____

6. Virī *ā mīlitibus* līberābuntur. _____

_____

Ablative of _____

7. Surgēmus *tertiā hōrā.* _____

_____

Ablative of _____

48 Lesson Forty-Eight
Ceres and Persephone Part One

Translate the first part of the story of Cerēs and Persephonē.

1. Nunc unum Deum adorant et Italī et Britannī. _____

_____

2. Sed olim Romanī multōs deōs, multās deās, adorābant. _____

_____

3. Dē deīs Romanīs fābulās narrābō. _____

_____

4. Cerēs erat dea frūmentī; in agrīs frūmentum, in prātīs herbam curābat. _____

_____

_____

5. Flāvum est frūmentum; flāvī erant deae capillī. _____

_____

6. Caerulea erat deae palla. _____

7. Persephonē erat fīlia deae. _____

_____

8. Cerēs fīliam cāram vehementer amābat. _____

_____

9. In īnsulā Siciliā Cerēs cum fīliā habitābat. _____

_____

10. Olīm Persephonē in prātīs errābat _____

_____

11. Cum puella aliae puellae errābant, nam locus herbōsus fuit grātus puellīs laetīs. _____

_____

_____

12. In prātō herbōsō puellae saltābant et cantābant. _____

_____

13. Multae rōsae, multa līlia, in prātīs erant _____

_____

14. Līlia alba puellās delectābant_____

15. Sed Plūtō, patruus puellae, Deae fīliam procul spectāvit et statim puellam vehementer amāvit.

_____

_____

16. Subitō equōs caeruleōs incitāvit et per prāta properāvit, et puellam perterritam raptāvit _____

_____

_____

17. Tum Persephonē, "O Cerēs," exclamat, "ubi es?" _____

_____

18. "Patruus meus fīliam tuam ad Inferōs portat." _____

_____

GLOSSARY

1. Britannus, -ī, *m.* — *a Briton (British person)*
2. cantō, -āre, -āvī, -ātum — *sing*
3. Cerēs, -eris, *f.* — *goddess of agriculture*
4. cūrō, -āre, -āvī, -ātum — *care for*
5. dē *(prep. w/abl.)* — *down from, from, about, concerning*
6. exclāmō, -āre, -āvī, -ātum — *exclaim, cry out*
7. habitō, -āre, -āvī, -ātum — *live in, inhabit*
8. Īnferī, -ōrum, *m.* — *The Underworld (Pluto's kingdom)*
9. īnsula, -ae, *f.* — *island*
10. Italus, -ī, *m.* — *an Italian*
11. laetus, -a, -um — *happy*
12. Mercurius, -ī, *m.* — *messenger of the gods*
13. nusquam — *nowhere*
14. olim — *once*
15. ōsculum, -ī, *n.* — *a kiss*
16. patruus, -ī, *m.* — *uncle*
17. Persephonē, -ēs, *f.* (Greek name) — *daughter of Cerēs (Roman name Proserpina)*
18. Plūtō, -ōnis, *m.* — *god of the underworld*
19. portō, -āre, -āvī, -ātum — *carry*
20. procul — *from afar*
21. properō, -āre, -āvī, -ātum — *hurry, hasten*
22. Rōmānus, -a, -um — *Roman (adj.)*
23. Rōmānus, -ī, *m.* — *a Roman*
24. saltō, -āre, -āvī, -ātum — *dance*
25. Sicilia, -ae, *f.* — *Sicily, an island off the coast of Italy*
26. ubi — *where*

Lesson Forty-Eight

R Unit Eight Review

A. *IS EA ID* ADJECTIVE REVIEW

List the adjective meanings for *is, ea, id*:

Singular — _____ , _____

Plural — _____ , _____

Now give the pronoun meanings for *is, ea, id*:

Singular — _____ , _____ , _____

Plural — _____

B. *IS EA ID* PRONOUN REVIEW

The demonstrative pronoun *is, ea, id* can be used in all five noun cases and has meanings for each case. Fill in the meanings in the chant below:

SINGULAR

CASE	Masc.	Translation	Fem.	Translation	Neut.	Translation
Nominative	is		ea		id	
Genitive	eius		eius		eius	
Dative	eī		eī		eī	
Accusative	eum		eam		id	
Ablative	eō		eā		eō	

Plural

CASE	Masc.	Translation	Fem.	Translation	Neut.	Translation
Nom.	eī		eae		ea	
Gen.	eōrum		eārum		eōrum	
Dat.	eīs		eīs		eīs	
Acc.	eōs		eās		ea	
Ab.	eīs		eīs		eīs	

C. *SUUS SUA SUUM* REVIEW

The genitive case for *is, ea, id* is not used to show possession. Instead, Latin relies on the adjective *suus, sua, suum* to show possession in third person. Write the meanings of this adjective.

Singular — _____ , _____ , _____

Plural — _____

Suus, sua, suum , like other adjectives, must match the noun it describes in what three ways?

_____ , _____ , _____

D. *IS EA ID* TRANSLATION REVIEW

Translate these sentences containing the demonstrative *is, ea, id* as both an adjective and a pronoun. Some sentences also contain forms of the third person possessive adjective *suus, sua, suum*.

1. Et Iūlia et Claudia suae magistrae līlia et rōsās carpsērunt. _____

_____

2. Magistra ab eīs delectābātur. _____

_____

3. Ea eās puellās laudāvit. _____

4. Claudius ea pōma edēbat. _____

5. Suae ūvae erant purpureae. _____

6. Iūlius in eō clivō errābat et is ūvās Claudī raptābat! _____

_____

7. Saxum et cēterī līberī Iūlium cēpērunt et is Claudiō suās ūvās dedit. _____

_____

_____

E. RELATIVE PRONOUN REVIEW

Fill in the meanings for the relative pronoun *qui, quae, quod*.

Singular

Case	Masc.	Translation	Fem.	Translation	Neut.	Translation
Nom.	quī		quae		quod	
Gen.	cuius		cuius		cuius	
Dat.	cui		cui		cui	
Acc.	quem		quam		quod	
Ab.	quō		quā		quō	

Plural

Case	Masc.	Translation	Fem.	Translation	Neut.	Translation
Nom.	quī		quae		quae	
Gen.	quōrum		quārum		quōrum	
Dat.	quibus		quibus		quibus	
Acc.	quōs		quās		quae	
Ab.	quibus		quibus		quibus	

F. RELATIVE PRONOUN TRANSLATION REVIEW

Translate sentences containing the relative pronoun *quī, quae, quod.* Circle the *antecedent* for each relative pronoun used.

1. Plūtō (quī rēx Inferōrum erat) Persephonē raptāvit. _____

_____

2. Cēterae puellae (quibuscum Persephonē errābat) nōn eam vīdērunt. _____

_____

3. Cerēs (quae nōn erat in Siciliā) fīliam suam vocābat (quae erat nusquam.) _____

_____

4. Mercūrius (quem Iūppiter ad Inferōs mīsit) puellam invenit. _____

_____

5. Cerēs (cui Mercūrius puellam apportāvit) fīliae suae ōsculum dedit. _____

_____

G. ABLATIVE COMPOSITION REVIEW

Translate these sentences containing some uses of the ablative case into Latin. Name the ablative being used.

1. Persephone was plucking those flowers *with her friends.* _____

_____

Ablative of _____

2. The girls were wandering *in the meadow.* _____

_____

Ablative of _____

3. Persephone was snatched *from the other girls.* _____

_____

Ablative of _____

4. Jupiter's words were given *by Mercury.* _____

_____

Ablative of _____

H. DERIVATIVE REVIEW

Write a paragraph in which you correctly use ten derivatives from Lists 15 and 16.

Underline the derivatives used.

_____

_____

_____

_____

_____

_____

_____

_____

_____

_____

_____

_____

_____

Unit 9

49 Lesson Forty-Nine
Review of Units 1-3

A. VOCABULARY REVIEW

Study Lists 1–6 for a few minutes, then try to translate the vocabulary below without looking.

Check your work and make corrections.

1. ignis _____
2. iuvō _____
3. equus _____
4. quod _____
5. caelum _____
6. dē _____
7. marītus _____
8. caveō _____
9. patria _____
10. altus _____
11. annus _____
12. hiems _____

13. sōl _____
14. amīcus _____
15. habeō _____
16. agitō _____
17. morbus _____
18. moneō _____
19. compleō _____
20. intrā _____
21. mundus _____
22. stō _____
23. ornō _____
24. vēr _____

B. SYNOPSIS

Do a synopsis of the verb *renovō, renovāre, renovāvī, renovātum* in the first person plural, active voice.

What conjugation is this verb? _____

What is the present stem? _____

What is the perfect stem? _____

TENSE	SYNOPSIS	TRANSLATION
present		
imperfect		
future		
perfect		
pluperfect		
future perfect		

Now do a synopsis of *renovō* in the first person plural, passive voice.

TENSE	SYNOPSIS	TRANSLATION
present		
imperfect		
future		

Do a synopsis of the verb *ardeō, ardēre, arsī, arsum* in the third person singular.

What conjugation is this verb? _____

What is the present stem? _____

What is the perfect stem? _____

TENSE	SYNOPSIS	TRANSLATION
present		
imperfect		
future		
perfect		
pluperfect		
future perfect		

Now do a synopsis of *ardeō* in the third person singular, passive voice.

TENSE	SYNOPSIS	TRANSLATION
present		
imperfect		
future		

C. IMPERATIVE REVIEW

Give the Latin singular and plural translations of the commands below.

WORD	SINGULAR COMMAND	PLURAL COMMAND
1. Lift the lid.	_____	_____
2. Guard against danger.	_____	_____
3. Tie the reins.	_____	_____

D. LINKING VERBS REVIEW

Review the linking verb in all six verb tenses (see Lesson 14). Then translate the linking verb forms below from memory.

1. es _____

2. erō _____

3. fuerat _____

4. fuerint _____

5. fuīmus _____

6. erās _____

7. est _____

8. eritis _____

9. fuerit _____

10. erant _____

11. fuistis _____

12. fuerimus _____

13. fuerātis _____

14. erit _____

15. sum _____

16. erāmus _____

17. fuistī _____

18. sumus _____

E. NOUN CASES REVIEW

Fill in the uses of the five noun cases below.

CASES USES

Nom.   _____ ,   _____ ,   _____

Gen.   _____ shown by _____, _____, _____

Dat.   _____ *or* shown by _____, _____

Acc.   _____ ,   _____

Ab.   List all the uses you can remember:

_____   _____   _____

_____   _____   _____

_____

F. NOUN-ADJECTIVE AGREEMENT REVIEW

Fill in information about noun-adjective agreement.

Adjectives must match the nouns they describe in *gender, number,* and *case.*

List the three *genders*: _____, _____, _____

List the two *numbers*: _____, _____

Do adjectives have to match the noun in *declension*? _____

List the PAIN words (nouns from first declension which are actually masculine).

P _____

A _____

I _____ (masc. or fem.)

N _____

G. TRANSLATION REVIEW

Translate the sentences below into Latin.

1. Saxum points out Julius's horse to (his) friends. _____

_____

2. The king will have given gifts to the men and women. _____

_____

3. We are able to tell the children stories at the fifth hour. _____

_____

4. You (pl.) will see the moon and stars in the sky. _____

_____

H. FOR FUN

Write a macaronic poem using at least ten Latin words from Lists 1-6.

_____

_____

_____

_____

_____

_____

_____

_____

_____

50 | Lesson Fifty
Review of Units 4-6

A. THIRD CONJUGATION REVIEW

Fill in the blanks about finding third conjugation verb stems.

To find the present stem of a third conjugation verb, remove the _____ ending from the

_____ principal part. The present stem is used for the _____ ,

_____, and _____ tenses.

To find the perfect stem of a third conjugation verb, remove the _____ ending from the

_____ principal part. The perfect stem is used for the _____ ,

_____, and _____ tenses.

B. SYNOPSIS

Do a verb synopsis for the third conjugation verb *pōnō, pōnere, posuī, positum* (which means "put" or "place") in the third person singular, active voice.

TENSE	SYNOPSIS	TRANSLATION
present		
imperfect		
future		
perfect		
pluperfect		
future perfect		

Now do a synopsis for the third conjugation i-stem verb, *fugiō, fugere, fūgī, fugītum* (meaning "flee from") in the third person plural.

TENSE	SYNOPSIS	TRANSLATION
present		
imperfect		
future		
perfect		
pluperfect		
future perfect		

C. CONJUGATION IDENTIFICATION REVIEW

Based on the first two principal parts of the verbs below, tell whether they are from first, second, third, or third i-stem conjugation.

VERB　　　　**CONJUGATION**

1. adfīgō, adfīgere　　_____

2. volō, volāre　　_____

3. capiō, capere　　_____

4. maneō, manēre　　_____

5. cadō, cadere　　_____

D. TENSE IDENTIFICATION REVIEW

Identify the tense of each third conjugation verb below and then translate.

VERB	TENSE	TRANSLATION
1. tēxerāmus	_____	_____
2. contendunt	_____	_____
3. fēcī	_____	_____
4. capiet	_____	_____
5. tangēbas	_____	_____
6. dīxeritis	_____	_____

E. THIRD DECLENSION CHANTS REVIEW

Decline the third declension nouns below. Highlight endings.

THIRD DECLENSION

senex	
senis	

THIRD DECLENSION I-STEM

fōns	
fontis	

THIRD DECLENSION NEUTER

lītus	
lītōris	

THIRD DECLENSION NEUTER I-STEM

mare	
maris	

F. THIRD DECLENSION IDENTIFICATION REVIEW

Below are the three rules for identifying third declension i-stem nouns. Using lists 7 — 12, give an example of each type of third i-stem noun.

Rule #1: If the nominative singular ends in *-is* or *-es*, and the genitive singular has the same number of syllables as the nominative, then the noun is an i-stem.

Example: _____

Rule #2: If the nominative singular ends in *-s* or *-x*, and its base ends in two consonants, then the noun is an i-stem.

Example: _____

Rule #3: If a noun is neuter and ends in *-al* or *-e* in the nominative singular, then the noun is an i-stem.

Example: _____

G. FOURTH DECLENSION CHANTS REVIEW

Decline the fourth and fourth declension neuter nouns below.

4TH DECLENSION

acus	
acūs	

4TH DECLENSION NEUTER

genu	
genūs	

H. FOURTH DECLENSION IDENTIFICATION REVIEW

Give the base for the nouns below and tell the declension of each noun.

NOUN	BASE	DECLENSION
1. vīnum, vīnī	_____	_____
2. glēba, glēbae	_____	_____
3. virgō, virgīnis	_____	_____
4. exitus, exitūs	_____	_____
5. fluvius, fluviī	_____	_____
6. cornū, cornūs	_____	_____

I. QUESTION REVIEW

Translate the questions below.

1. Ponetne rēx statuam deae in templō trāns fluvium? _____

_____

2. Nonne pānem ēdistī et vīnum potāvistī cum fīliā rēgis? _____

_____

_____

3. Num calor cēram liquefēcerat? _____

_____

4. Quis contendēbat cum Minervā? _____

_____

5. Quid Arachnē nēvit? _____

_____

6. Quando līberī cēnam edent?_____

_____

7. Quot vetulae textum texunt?_____

_____

8. Ubi erās? _____

J. IMPERATIVE REVIEW

Translate the commands below into English. Tell whether the command is from first, second, or third conjugation and whether it is singular or plural.

COMMAND	TRANSLATION	S/P	CONJ.
1. Mutā colōrem.	_____	___	_____
2. Pone in mensā pānem.	_____	___	_____
3. Surgite.	_____	___	_____
4. Manē in templō.	_____	___	_____
5. Volāte.	_____	___	_____
6. Docēte.	_____	___	_____

K. VOCATIVE REVIEW

Give the vocative form for each noun below.

NOUN VOCATIVE FORM

1. Iūlius   _____

2. Marcus   _____

3. Iūlia   _____

4. puellae   _____

5. puerī   _____

L. DEMONSTRATIVE ADJECTIVE REVIEW

Translate sentences below containing the demonstrative adjectives *hic* and *ille*.

1. Hī virī illum vīnum cum hāc cenā potāvērunt. _____

_____

2. Haec māter huic fīliae illam vestem dat. _____

_____

3. Illa turris aedificābitur ā hōc sene.* _____

_____

*Which ablative is being used here? _____

M. DERIVATIVE REVIEW

Write a story using at least twenty derivatives from Lists 7-12.

_____

_____

_____

_____

_____

_____

_____

_____

_____

_____

Lesson Fifty 315

51 Lesson Fifty-One
Review: Lists 13-16 & Units 7-8

A. FOURTH CONJUGATION SYNOPSIS REVIEW

Do a synopsis of the fourth conjugation verb *dormiō, dormīre, dormīvī, dormītum* in the first person plural, active voice.

TENSE	SYNOPSIS	TRANSLATION
present		
imperfect		
future		
perfect		
pluperfect		
future perfect		

What is the present stem of *dormiō*? _____

What is the perfect stem of *dormiō*? _____

B. FIFTH DECLENSION CHANT REVIEW

Decline the fifth declension noun *res, rei*.

rēs	
rēī	

C. PERSONAL PRONOUNS TRANSLATION REVIEW

Translate the *personal pronouns only* in the English sentences below. Make sure to identify how the pronoun is used. Is it a subject noun, direct object, or indirect object? Is it singular or plural? Choose from forms of **egō** *(I, me)*, **tū** *(you sing.)*, **nōs** *(we, us)*, **vōs** *(you plural)*, or **is, ea, id** *(he, she, it, they)*. Some sentences explain the pronoun in parentheses. Examples are given.

N.B. With **is, ea, id** pay attention to the gender of the noun represented by the pronoun.

   Example 1: **You sing.** will give **her** the lily. <u>**Tū, eī**</u>

   Example 2: **They (girls)** decorate **it (a small boat)** with roses. <u>**Eae , eam**</u>

1. **We** did sail **them (ships)** to shore. _____ _____

2. **I** had assembled **you all**. _____ _____

3. **He** will reach **it (the kingdom)** during the day. _____ _____

4. The king gives **them (the young men)** crowns. _____

Challenge sentence: **They (the sailors)** send a message to Greece. _____

Now translate the sentences above into Latin. See the examples below:

   Example 1: Tū eī līlium dābit.

   Example 2: Eae eam rōsīs ornant.

1. _____

2. _____

3. _____

4. _____

Challenge: _____

Next, use *is, ea, id* as a demonstrative adjective and translate the underlined words only after considering the examples:

> You (sing.) will give **this** girl the lily. *eī puellae*
> **These** girls decorate **that** small boat with roses. *Eae puellae, eam naviculam*

1. We did sail **those** ships to shore. _____

2. He will reach **that** kingdom during the day. _____

3. The king gives **these** young men crowns. _____

Finally, translate the underlined phrases only, using the possessive pronoun *suus, sua, suum* (his, her, its, their). *Suus, sua, suum* must match the noun it describes in gender, number, and case.

> You (sing.) will give **his girl** the lily. *suae puellae*
> **Their girls** will decorate **his small boat** with roses. *Suae puellae, suam nāviculam*

1. We did sail **his ships** to shore. _____

2. He will reach **their kingdom** during the day. _____

3. The king gives **his young men** crowns. _____

D. ABLATIVE TRANSLATION REVIEW

Translate the sentences below containing the ablative case. Tell which ablative is being used.

Choices are ablative of: place where, place from which, time when, time during, means, manner, personal agent, separation, and accompaniment.

1. Iūlia et Claudia ūvās carpunt cum Saxō._____

_____

Ablative of _____

2. Exercitus rēgnum ab impetū līberāvit. _____

_____

Ablative of _____

3. Nautae lītus pervenient rēmīs. _____

_____

Ablative of _____

4. Munīmus templum in īnsulā._____

_____

Ablative of _____

E. RELATIVE PRONOUN TRANSLATION REVIEW

Translate sentences containing the relative pronun *quī, quae, quod.*

1. Claudia (quae in prātō errābat) delectābātur ā līliīs purpureīs. _____

_____

2. Nāvis (quam nautae navigāvērunt) erat magna. _____

_____

3. Mīlēs (cuius exercitus portum oppugnāverat) lītus pervēnit. _____

_____

F. DERIVATIVE REVIEW

List ten English derivatives and their Latin origins on the lines below.

	DERIVATIVE	LATIN ORIGIN
1.	_____	_____
2.	_____	_____
3.	_____	_____
4.	_____	_____
5.	_____	_____
6.	_____	_____
7.	_____	_____
8.	_____	_____
9.	_____	_____
10.	_____	_____

ACTIVITY
PAGES

MACARONIC FAIRY TALE

Write a macaronic fairy tale using at least ten Latin words from List One. <u>Underline</u> the Latin words.

_____

_____

_____

_____

_____

_____

_____

_____

_____

_____

_____

_____

_____

_____

_____

Activity Page

Activity Two

CROSSWORD PUZZLE

The ACROSS and DOWN clues are given in English. Fill in the crossword with the Latin translations.

ACROSS

3. Chariot
4. And
7. Torch
8. See
11. Horse
12. Because
13. Drive
15. Liver
16. Flame

DOWN

1. Vulture
2. Burn
5. Hold
6. Gift
9. Sit
10. Tie
14. Weapon
15. Anger

Activity Page 327

WORD SEARCH PUZZLE

Find each word in the grid. Words can go horizontally, vertically, and diagonal as well as backwards or forwards.

```
M  U  S  S  O  P  A  R  U  C
A  I  D  I  V  N  I  H  B  E
D  F  G  O  U  A  N  E  O  P
C  A  X  M  O  R  B  U  S  S
A  B  C  R  E  T  A  R  F  D
E  U  A  V  A  R  I  T  I  A
L  L  K  S  U  P  O  S  E  A
U  A  A  U  S  C  U  L  T  O
M  G  E  D  A  R  T  N  O  C
B  A  P  P  O  R  T  O  C  V
```

Fabula	Vox	Morbus	Contra
Poena	Avaritia	Possum	Ausculto
Caelum	Invidia	Apporto	Aesopus
Frater	Cura	De	

Activity Four

CARTOON

Imagine that a husband and wife find a box. Draw a cartoon about what happens when they open the box. Use at least ten Latin words from List Four in the conversation bubbles.

A Activity Five

DERIVATIVE STORY

Using at least ten English derivatives from List Five, write a story in which you get to drive Apollo's chariot across the sky.

_____

_____

_____

_____

_____

_____

_____

_____

_____

_____

_____

_____

_____

_____

 Activity Six

DRAWING

Draw Apollo's palace. Represent the seasons, years, months, and days as persons standing around Apollo on his throne. Label in Latin. This activity relates to Lesson 18, a myth about Phaethon and the Sun God's Chariot.

Activity Seven

MACARONIC POEM

Write a poem about a feast. Use at least ten Latin words from List Seven and <u>underline</u> the Latin words.

_____

_____

_____

_____

_____

_____

_____

_____

_____

_____

_____

_____

_____

_____

_____

_____

Activity Page

Activity Eight

CROSSWORD PUZZLE

The ACROSS and DOWN clues are given in English. Fill in the crossword with the Latin translations.

ACROSS

2. Hunger
3. Swallow
5. Father
7. Elder
8. Fish
10. Across
13. Hide
14. Stone
16. King
17. Throat

DOWN

1. Greedy
2. Fountain
4. Garment
6. Touch
8. Bread
9. River
11. Statue
12. Wail
15. Carry

 **Activity Nine**

MAP

Draw a map of an island. Include at least eight items from List Nine on your map and label the pictures in Latin.

WORD SCRAMBLE

Unscramble each Latin word below, and give the English translation.

	Latin Word	**English Translation**
1. tugo	_____	_____
2. rloac	_____	_____
3. somr	_____	_____
4. rsmuu	_____	_____
5. rbiel	_____	_____
6. utust	_____	_____
7. essp	_____	_____
8. dlusu	_____	_____
9. truusa	_____	_____
10. nmuefl	_____	_____

A Activity Eleven

DERIVATIVE STORY

Rewrite a fairytale, fable, or other familiar story using at least ten English derivatives from List Eleven. <u>Underline</u> derivatives used.

_____

_____

_____

_____

_____

_____

_____

_____

_____

_____

_____

_____

_____

_____

_____

_____

Activity Twelve

MACARONIC STORY

Write a macaronic story about a spider who spins in different colors. Add some illustrations in the extra space on the right.

_____

_____

_____

_____

_____

_____

_____

_____

_____

_____

_____

_____

_____

_____

_____

_____

_____

_____

_____

_____

_____

_____

_____

_____

_____

_____

_____

_____

_____

_____

_____

_____

_____

_____

_____

CARTOON

Draw a cartoon about a sailor. Use at least ten Latin words from List Thirteen and <u>underline</u> the words used.

Activity Fourteen

WORD SEARCH PUZZLE

Find each word in the grid. Words can go horizontally, vertically, and diagonal as well as backwards or forwards.

```
V  A  N  C  O  R  A  Q  S  O
E  U  C  S  S  A  B  V  N  I
L  O  L  E  O  L  M  A  E  T
L  C  I  I  R  U  U  S  C  O
U  A  B  D  E  C  L  U  S  P
S  R  E  I  H  I  O  I  E  H
T  D  R  R  E  V  C  T  L  N
E  C  O  E  X  A  F  N  U  Y
S  K  Y  M  D  N  L  U  D  C
C  O  R  O  N  A  O  N  A  D
```

Columba	Nuntius	Corona	Navicula
Vellus	Draco	Heros	Potio
Meridies	Ancora	Adulescens	Libero

Activity Fifteen

CROSSWORD PUZZLE

The ACROSS and DOWN clues are given in English. Fill in the crossword with the Latin translations.

ACROSS

2. From all sides
4. While
5. Grass
7. Grassy
10. Break
11. Purple
14. Hill
15. Plant
16. Another
17. Immediately
18. Fruit

DOWN

1. Delight
2. Grape
3. Because
4. Desire
6. Red
8. Precious
9. Your (pl.)
12. Meadow
13. Lily

WORD SCRAMBLE

Unscramble each Latin word below, and give the English translation.

	Latin Word	English Translation
1. ēpss	_____	_____
2. ulan	_____	_____
3. ōbitsu	_____	_____
4. citinō	_____	_____
5. pillacu	_____	_____
6. tāgrus	_____	_____
6. īterēc	_____	_____
8. paratō	_____	_____
9. cofus	_____	_____
10. timtō	_____	_____

REFERENCE
PAGES

Verb Chants

FIRST CONJUGATION

amō	amāmus
amās	amātis
amat	amant

SECOND CONJUGATION

videō	vidēmus
vidēs	vidētis
videt	vident

THIRD CONJUGATION

dūcō	dūcimus
ducis	ducitis
ducit	ducunt

FOURTH CONJUGATION

audiō	audīmus
audīs	audītis
audit	audiunt

LINKING VERBS (PRESENT TENSE)

sum	sumus
es	estis
est	sunt

PRESENT TENSE VERB ENDINGS

-ō	-mus
-s	-tis
-t	-nt

FUTURE TENSE VERB ENDINGS

-bō	-bimus
-bis	-bitis
-bit	-bunt

IMPERFECT TENSE VERB ENDINGS

-bam	-bāmus
-bās	-bātis
-bat	-bant

PERFECT TENSE VERB ENDINGS

-ī	-imus
-istī	-istis
-it	-ērunt

FUTURE PERFECT TENSE VERB ENDINGS

-erō	-erimus
-eris	-eritis
-erit	-erint

Verb Chants

POSSUM CHANT

possum	possumus
potes	potestis
potest	possunt

PRESENT PASSIVE VERB ENDINGS

-r	-mur
-ris	-minī
-tur	-ntur

IMPERFECT TENSE VERB ENDINGS

-bār	-bāmur
-bāris	-bāminī
-bātur	-bāntur

PLUPERFECT TENSE VERB ENDINGS

-eram	-erāmus
-erās	-erātis
-erat	-erant

FUTURE PASSIVE VERB ENDINGS

-bor	-bimur
-beris	-biminī
-bitur	-buntur

PERFECT TENSE VERB ENDINGS

-ī	-imus
-istī	-istis
-it	-ērunt

® Noun Chants

Noun chant endings do not have meanings in the same way that verb endings do. Instead, noun endings can tell what part of speech a word is, such as the subject noun. Like verbs, nouns have different families which are called *declensions*.

FIRST DECLENSION

-a	-ae
-ae	-ārum
-ae	-īs
-am	-ās
-ā	-īs

SECOND DECLENSION

-us	-ī
-ī	-ōrum
-ō	-īs
-um	-ōs
-ō	-īs

SECOND DECLENSION NEUTER

-um	-a
-ī	-ōrum
-ō	-īs
-um	-a
-ō	-īs

THIRD DECLENSION

-x	-ēs
-is	-um
-ī	-ibus
-em	-ēs
-e	-ibus

THIRD DECLENSION I-STEM

-is	-ēs
-is	-ium
-ī	-ibus
-em	-ēs
-e	-ibus

THIRD DECLENSION NEUTER

-x	-a
-is	-um
-ī	-ibus
-x	-a
-e	-ibus

Noun Chants

THIRD DECLENSION NEUTER I-STEM

-x	-ia
-is	-ium
-ī	-ibus
-x	-ia
-ī	-ibus

FOURTH DECLENSION NEUTER

-ū	-ua
-ūs	-uum
-ū	-ibus
-ū	-ua
-ū	-ibus

FOURTH DECLENSION

-us	-ūs
-ūs	-uum
-uī	-ibus
-um	-ūs
-ū	-ibus

FIFTH DECLENSION

-ēs	-ēs
-ēī	-ērum
-ēi	-ēbus
-em	-ēs
-ē	-ēbus

DEMONSTRATIVE PRONOUNS

Memorize the chants across, not down.

SINGULAR — THIS

hic	haec	hoc
huius	huius	huius
huic	huic	huic
hunc	hanc	hoc
hōc	hāc	hōc

PLURAL — THESE

hī	hae	haec
hōrum	hārum	hōrum
hīs	hīs	hīs
hōs	hās	haec
hīs	hīs	hīs

PERSONAL PRONOUNS

Memorize the chants down, not across.

1. SINGULAR — FIRST PERSON (I/ME)

ego
meī
mihi
mē
mē

3. PLURAL — FIRST PERSON (WE)

nōs
nostrum
nōbis
nōs
nōbīs

2. SINGULAR — SECOND PERSON (YOU)

tū
tuī
tibi
tē
tē

4. PLURAL — SECOND PERSON (YOU ALL)

vōs
vestrum
vōbīs
vōs
vōbīs

Pronoun Chants

DEMONSTRATIVE PRONOUNS CONTINUED

Memorize the chants across, not down.

SINGULAR — THAT

→

M	F	N
ille	illa	illud
illīus	illīus	illīus
illī	illī	illī
illum	illam	illud
illō	illā	illō

PLURAL — THOSE

→

M	F	N
illī	illae	illa
illōrum	illārum	illōrum
illīs	illīs	illīs
illōs	illās	illa
illīs	illīs	illīs

SINGULAR — THIS, THAT, HE, SHE, IT

M	F	N
is	ea	id
eius	eius	eius
eī	eī	eī
eum	eam	id
eō	eā	eō

PLURAL — THESE, THOSE, THEY

M	F	N
eī	eae	ea
eōrum	eārum	eōrum
eīs	eīs	eīs
eōs	eās	ea
eīs	eīs	eīs

FIVE NOUN CASES

Nominative	→	NO
Genitive	→	GENTLE
Dative	→	DAD
Accusative	→	ACCUSES
Ablative	→	APPLES

HOW TO FIND THE NOUN BASE

Don't try to change the case
      until you find the base.
The genitive case
      is the place to find the base.
And I forgot to mention
      it also shows declension!

LATIN ACTIVE VERB TENSE CHART I

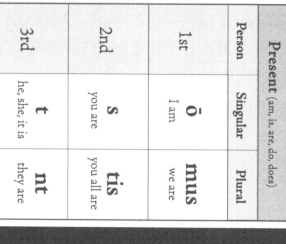

Present (am, is, are, do, does)

Person	Singular	Plural
1st	**ō** I am	**mus** we are
2nd	**s** you are	**tis** you all are
3rd	**t** he, she, it is	**nt** they are

Imperfect (was, were, used to)

Person	Singular	Plural
1st	**bam** I was	**bāmus** we were
2nd	**bās** you were	**bātis** you all were
3rd	**bat** he, she, it was	**bant** they were

Future (will, shall)

Person	Singular	Plural
1st	**bō** I will	**bimus** we will
2nd	**bis** you will	**bitis** you all will
3rd	**bit** he, she, it will	**bunt** they will

LATIN NOUN ENDINGS CHART I

CASE KEY	NOM: NOMINATIVE	GEN: GENITIVE	DAT: DATIVE	ACC: ACCUSATIVE	ABL: ABLATIVE

1st Declension

Case	Singular	Plural
Nom	a	ae
Gen	ae	ārum
Dat	ae	īs
Acc	am	ās
Abl	ā	īs

2nd Declension

Case	Singular	Plural
Nom	us	ī
Gen	ī	ōrum
Dat	ō	īs
Acc	um	ōs
Abl	ō	īs

2nd Declension Neuter

Case	Singular	Plural
Nom	um	a
Gen	ī	ōrum
Dat	ō	īs
Acc	um	a
Abl	ō	īs

3rd Declension

Case	Singular	Plural
Nom	x	ēs
Gen	is	um
Dat	ī	ibus
Acc	em	ēs
Abl	e	ibus

3rd Declension Neuter

Case	Singular	Plural
Nom	x	a
Gen	is	um
Dat	ī	ibus
Acc	x	a
Abl	e	ibus

Perfect (-ed, has, have, did)

Person	Singular	Plural
1st	ī I have	imus we have
2nd	istī you have	istis you all have
3rd	it he, she, it has	ērunt they have

Pluperfect (had)

Person	Singular	Plural
1st	eram I had	erāmus we had
2nd	erās you had	erātis you all had
3rd	erat he, she, it had	erant they had

Future Perfect (will have, shall have)

Person	Singular	Plural
1st	erō I will have	erimus we will have
2nd	eris you will have	eritis you all will have
3rd	erit he, she, it will have	erint they will have

LATIN NOUN ENDINGS CHART II

3rd Declension i-Stem Neuter

Case	Singular	Plural
Nom	x	ia
Gen	is	ium
Dat	ī	ibus
Acc	x	ia
Abl	ī	ibus

5th Declension

Case	Singular	Plural
Nom	ēs	ēs
Gen	ēī	ērum
Dat	ēī	ēbus
Acc	em	ēs
Abl	ē	ēbus

4th Declension Neuter

Case	Singular	Plural
Nom	ū	ua
Gen	ūs	uum
Dat	ū	ibus
Acc	ū	ua
Abl	ū	ibus

3rd Declension i-Stem

Case	Singular	Plural
Nom	is	ēs
Gen	is	ium
Dat	ī	ibus
Acc	em	ēs
Abl	e	ibus

4th Declension

Case	Singular	Plural
Nom	us	ūs
Gen	ūs	uum
Dat	uī	ibus
Acc	um	ūs
Abl	ū	ibus

 **R** Memory Work

INTRODUCTION TO THE AENEID, LINES 1-7

Arma virumque cano, Troiae qui primus ab oris
Italiam fato profugus Lavinaque venit
litora–multum ille et terris iactatus et alto
vi superum, saevae memorem Iunonis ob iram
multa quoque et bello passus, dum conderet urbem
inferretque deos Latio–genus unde Latinum
Albanique patres atque altae moenia Romae.

Translation (The Aeneid)

Arms and the man I sing, the first who came,
Compelled by fate, an exile out of Troy,
To Italy and the Laviniam coast,
Much buffeted on land and on the deep
By violence and the gods, through that long rage,
That lasting hate, of Juno's. And he suffered
Much, also, in war, till he should build his town
And bring his gods to Latium, whence, in time,
The Latin race, the Alban fathers, rose
And the great walls of everlasting Rome.

Memory Work

SYMBOLUM APOSTOLORUM (THE APOSTLE'S CREED)

Credo in Deum Patrem omnipotentem, Creatorem caeli et terrae.

Et in Iesus Christum, Filium eius unicum, Dominum nostrum,
qui conceptus est de Spiritu Sancto, natus ex Maria Virgine,
passus sub Pontio Pilato, crucifixus, mortuus, et sepultus,
descendit ad inferos, tertia die resurrexit a mortuis,
ascendit ad caelos, sedet ad dexteram Dei Patris omnipotentis,
inde venturus est iudicare vivos et mortuos.

Credo in Spiritum Sanctum, sanctam Ecclesiam catholicam, sanctorum communionem,
remissionem peccatorum, carnis resurrectionem, vitam aeteram. Amen.

Translation (The Apostle's Creed)

I believe in God the Father Almighty; Maker of heaven and earth,

and in Jesus Christ, His only begotten Son, our Lord.
He was conceived by the Holy Ghost, and born of the virgin, Mary.
He suffered under Pontius Pilate, was crucified, died, and was buried.
He descended into Hades. On the third day He rose again from the dead,
ascended into Heaven, and sits at the right hand of God the Father Almighty;
from thence He will come to judge the living and the dead.

I believe in the Holy Ghost, the holy catholic Church, the communion of saints,
the forgiveness of sins, the resurrection of the body, and the life everlasting. Amen.

R Review—Memory Work

CANTICUM DAVID

[1] Dominus pascit me nihil mihi deerit

[2] in pascuis herbarum adclinavit me super aquas refectionis enutrivit me

[3] animam meam refecit duxit me per semitas iustitiae propter nomen suum

[4] sed et si ambulavero in valle mortis non timebo malum quoniam tu mecum es virga tua et baculus tuus ipsa consolabuntur me

[5] pones coram me mensam ex adverso hostium meorum inpinguasti oleo caput meum calix meus inebrians

[6] sed et benignitas et misericordia subsequetur me omnibus diebus vitae meae et habitabo in domo Domini in longitudine dierum

Translation (A Psalm of David)

[1] The Lord is my shepherd; I shall not want.

[2] He makes me to lie down in green pastures; He leads me beside the still waters.

[3] He restores my soul; He leads me in the paths of righteousness For His name's sake.

[4] Yea, though I walk through the valley of the shadow of death, I will fear no evil; For You are with me; Your rod and Your staff, they comfort me.

[5] You prepare a table before me in the presence of my enemies; You anoint my head with oil; My cup runs over.

[6] Surely goodness and mercy shall follow me All the days of my life; And I will dwell in the house of the Lord forever.

Ⓡ Review—Memory Work

PATER NOSTER

[1] Pater noster, qui es in caelis,

[2] sanctificetur Nomen Tuum.

[3] adveniat regnum Tuum;

[4] fiat voluntas Tua

[5] sicut in caelo et in terra.

[6] Panem nostrum cotidianum da nobis hodie,

[7] et dimitte nobis debita nostra,

[8] Sicut et nos dimittimus debitoribus nostris,

[9] et ne nos inducas in tentationem,

[10] sed libera nos a malo.

[11] Amen.

Translation (The Lord's Prayer)

[1] Our Father who art in heaven,

[2] hallowed be Thy name.

[3] Thy kingdom come.

[4] Thy will be done

[5] on earth as it is in heaven.

[6] Give us this day our daily bread,

[7] and forgive us our trespasses,

[8] as we forgive those who trespass against us,

[9] and lead us not into temptation,

[10] but deliver us from evil.

[11] Amen.

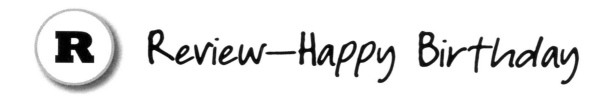

Review—Happy Birthday

FELIX DIES NATALIS

Tibi diem natalem felicem,
Tibi diem natalem felicem,
Diem natalem felicem carus/cara (name),
Tibi diem natalem felicem!

Translation (Happy Birthday)

Happy birthday to you,
Happy birthday to you,
Happy birthday, dear (name),
Happy birthday to you!

R Review—Memory Work

CREATIO

[1] In principio creavit Deus caelum et terram

[2] terra autem erat inanis et vacua et tenebrae super faciem abyssi et spiritus Dei ferebatur super aquas

[3] dixitque Deus fiat lux et facta est lux

[4] et vidit Deus lucem quod esset bona et divisit lucem ac tenebras

[5] appellavitque lucem diem et tenebras noctem factumque est vespere et mane dies unus

Translation (Creation, Genesis 1:1–5)

[1] In the beginning God created the heavens and the earth.

[2] The earth was without form, and void; and darkness was on the face of the deep. And the Spirit of God was hovering over the face of the waters.

[3] Then God said, "Let there be light"; and there was light.

[4] And God saw the light, that it was good; and God divided the light from the darkness.

[5] God called the light Day, and the darkness He called Night. So the evening and the morning were the first day.

MAGNIFICAT

[46] et ait Maria magnificat anima mea Dominum

[47] et exultavit spiritus meus in Deo salutari meo

[48] quia respexit humilitatem ancillae suae ecce enim ex hoc beatam me dicent omnes generationes

[49] quia fecit mihi magna qui potens est et sanctum nomen eius

[50] et misericordia eius in progenies et progenies timentibus eum

[51] fecit potentiam in brachio suo dispersit superbos mente cordis sui

[52] deposuit potentes de sede et exaltavit humiles

[53] esurientes implevit bonis et divites dimisit inanes

[54] suscepit Israhel puerum suum memorari misericordiae

[55] sicut locutus est ad patres nostros Abraham et semini eius in saecula

Translation (Song of Mary, Luke 1:46–55))

[46] And Mary said: "My soul magnifies the Lord,

[47] And my spirit has rejoiced in God my Savior.

[48] For He has regarded the lowly state of His maidservant; For behold, henceforth all generations will call me blessed.

[49] For He who is mighty has done great things for me, And holy is His name.

[50] And His mercy is on those who fear Him From generation to generation.

[51] He has shown strength with His arm; He has scattered the proud in the imagination of their hearts.

[52] He has put down the mighty from their thrones, And exalted the lowly.

[53] He has filled the hungry with good things, And the rich He has sent away empty.

[54] He has helped His servant Israel, In remembrance of His mercy,

[55] As He spoke to our fathers, To Abraham and to his seed forever."

Review—Present Verb Stem Flower 1st & 2nd Conjugations

From *Logos Latin 3*, Lesson Seventeen.

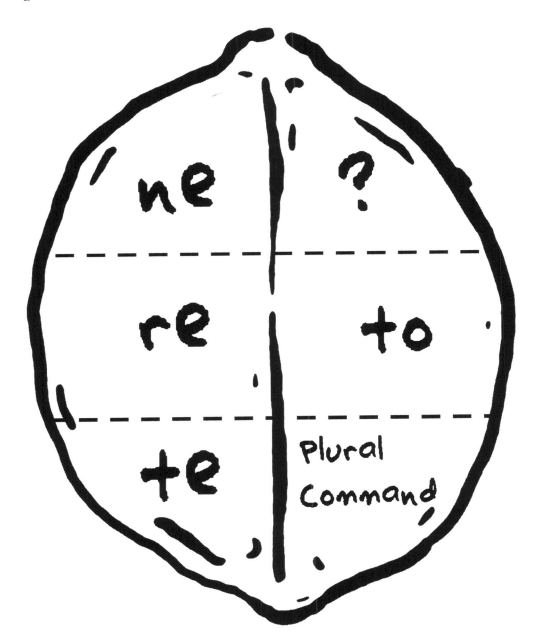

R Ordinal Number Comparison Chart

	LATIN	FRENCH	ITALIAN	SPANISH	ROMANIAN
0	nihil	zéro	zero	cero	zero
1	ūnus	un	uno	uno	unu
2	duo	deux	due	dos	doi
3	trēs	trois	tre	tres	trei
4	quattuor	quatre	quattro	cuatro	patru
5	quīnque	cinq	cinque	cinco	cinci
6	sex	six	sei	seis	şase
7	septem	sept	sette	siete	şapte
8	octō	huit	otto	ocho	opt
9	novem	neuf	nove	nueve	nouă
10	decem	dix	dieci	diez	zece
11	ūndecim	onze	undici	once	unsprezece
12	duodēcim	douze	dodici	doce	douăsprezece
100	centum	cent	cento	ciento	o suta
1000	mille	mille	mille	mil	o mie

G Glossary—Latin to English

The number in parentheses indicates the list in which the word is introduced. Some words from *ogos Latin 1, 2,* and *3* appear only in Review Lists. These words are indicated by the abbreviation *Rv.*.

A
ā, ab (prep. with abl.), *from, away from (Rv. 2)*
aciēs, acieī, f., *line of battle, straight line (14)*
acus, -ūs, f., *needle (11)*
acūtus, -a, -um, *sharp (11)*
ad (prep. with acc.), *to, toward (2)*
adfīgō, adfīgere, adfīxī, adfīxum, *fasten to, affix (9)*
adōrō, -āre, -āvī, -ātum, *worship (16)*
adulēscēns, adulēscentis, m., *young man (14)*
adventus, -ūs, m., *arrival, approach (11)*
aeger, aegra, aegrum, *sick (Rv. 10)*
aer, aeris, m., *air (4)*
aedificium, -ī, n., *building (Rv. 9)*
aedificō, -āre, -āvī, -ātum, *build (9)*
Aesōpus, Aesōpī, m., *Aesop (Rv. 3)*
aestās, aestātis, f., *summer (6)*
ager, agrī, m., *field (15)*
agitō, -āre, -āvī, -ātum, *drive (2)*
ala, -ae, f., *wing (4)*
albus, -a, -um, *white (Rv. 6)*
alius, -a, -ud, *other, another (15)*
altus, -a, -um, *high, deep (5)*
ambulō, -āre, -āvī, -ātum, *walk (Rv. 2)*
amīca, -ae, f., *female friend (Rv. 11)*
amīcus, -ī, m., *friend (1)*
amō, -āre, -āvi, -ātum, *love, like (1)*
ancora, -ae, f., *anchor (14)*
annus, -ī, m., *year (6)*
Apollō, Apollinis, m., *sun god (6)*
apportō, -āre, -āvī, -ātum, *bring (3)*
aqua, -ae, f., *water (Rv. 8)*

arānea, -ae, f., *spider (12)*
arbor, arboris, f., *tree (Rv. 7)*
arca, -ae, f., *chest, box (4)*
arceō, -ēre, arcuī, ---------, *shut in (4)*
ardeō, -ēre, arsī, arsum, *burn, blaze (2)*
argenteus, -a, -um, *silver, silvery (5)*
argentum, -ī, n., *silver (5)*
ariēs, ariētis, m., *ram (14)*
arō, -āre, -āvī, -ātum, *plow (1)*
ars, artis, f., *skill (11)*
astrum -ī, n., *constellation (5)*
audācia, -ae, f., *boldness (Rv. 13)*
audeō, -ēre, ausus sum, *dare (11)*
audiō, -īre, -īvī, -ītum, *hear (13)*
aureus, -a, -um, *golden (5)*
aurum, -ī, n., *gold (5)*
auscultō, -āre, -āvī, -ātum, *listen to (Rv. 12)*
autumna, -ae, f., *autumn (6)*
avāritia, -ae, f., *greed (3)*
avārus, -a, -um, *greedy (8)*
avia, -ae, f., *grandmother (Rv. 12)*
avis, -is, f., *bird (9)*
avunculus, -ī, m., *uncle (mother's brother) (Rv. 14)*

B
benevolentia, -ae, f., *goodwill, kindness (3)*
bēstiola, -ae, f., *insect (Rv. 12)*
bonus, -a, -um, *good (Rv. 6)*
bracchium, -ī, n., *arm (10)*

C
cadō, -ere, cecīdī, casum, *fall, drop (10)*
caelum, -ī, n., *sky, heaven (3)*

caeruleus, -a, -um, *blue (12)*

calor, calōris, m., *heat (10)*

campus, -ī, m., *plain (15)*

canō, -ere, cecinī, cantum, *play (on an instrument; used with ablative) (Rv. 12)*

capillus, -ī, m., *hair (often plural) (16)*

capiō, -ere, cēpī, captum, *capture (9)*

carcer, carceris, m., *prison (9)*

carpō, -ere, carpsī, carptum, *pluck (7)*

cārus, -a, -um, *dear (15)*

castellum, -i, n., *castle (Rv. 9)*

caveō, -ēre, cāvī, cautum, *guard against, beware (4)*

celeritās, celeritātis, f., *speed (12)*

cēna, -ae, f., *dinner, meal (7)*

cēra, -ae, f., *wax (10)*

cēterī, -ae, -a, *the rest (of) (16)*

cognoscō, -ere, cognōvī, cognitum, *recognize (7)*

cibus, -ī, m., *food (7)*

circā (prep. with acc.), *around (10)*

citus, -a, -um, *fast, swift (Rv. 6)*

clamō, -āre, -āvī, -ātum, *shout (10)*

Claudius, -ī, m., *Claudius or Claude, friend of Julius (Rv. 1)*

Claudia, -ae, f., *Claudia, sister of Claudius and friend of Julia (Rv. 1)*

clīvus, -ī, m., *hill (15)*

cōgitātiō, cōgitātiōnis, f., *idea (9)*

color, colōris, m., *color (12)*

columba, -ae, f., *dove (Rv. 14)*

coma, -ae, f., *hair, leaves of a tree (Rv. 16)*

compleō, -ēre, complēvi, complētum, *fill, fill up (4)*

consīlium, -ī, n., *advice, plan (12)*

contendō, -ere, contendī, contentum, *contend, compete (11)*

contra (prep. with abl.) *against (3)*

conveniō, -īre, -vēnī, -ventum, *assemble (13)*

cornū, -us, n., *horn (animal or trumpet) (12)*

corōna, -ae, f., *crown (14)*

corpus, corporis, n., *body (9)*

creō, -āre, -āvī, -ātum, *create (1)*

cupiō, cupere, cupīvī, cupītum, *wish, want, desire (Rv. 15)*

cūra, -ae, f., *care, worry (3)*

currō, -ere, cucurrī, cursum, *run (Rv. 8)*

currus, -ūs, m., *chariot (2)*

D dē (prep. with abl.), *about, concerning, down from, from (3)*

dea, -ae, f., *goddess (11)*

decimus, -a, -um, *tenth (Rv. 6)*

dēfendo, -ere, dēfendī, dēfēnsum, *defend (14)*

dēfessus, -a, -um, *tired (Rv. 6)*

delectō, -āre, -āvī, -ātum, *delight (15)*

dēmōnstrō, -āre, -āvi, -ātum, *show, point out (1)*

dens, dentis, m., *tooth (14)*

desiderō, -āre, -āvī, -ātum, *miss, want (15)*

dēvōrō, -āre, -āvi, -ātum *devour, swallow (1)*

deus, -ī, m., *god (1)*

diēs, diēī, m., *day (6)*

dīcō, -ere, dīxī, dictum, *say, speak, tell (7)*

diū, *for a long time (Rv. 11)*

dīvīnus, -a, -um, *divine (16)*

dō, -āre, dedī, datum, *give (1)*

doceō, -ēre, docuī, doctum, *teach (10)*

domus, -ūs, f., *house, home (Rv. 5)*

dōnum, -ī, n., *gift (2)*

dormiō, -īre, -īvī, -ītum, *sleep (13)*

draco, dracōnis, m., *dragon (14)*

dūcō, -ere, dūxī, ductum, *lead (7)*

dum, *while (Rv. 15)*

E ē, ex (prep. with abl.), *out of, from (Rv. 2)*

edō, -ere, ēdī, ēsum, *eat (7)*

equus, -ī, m., *horse (2)*

errō, -āre, -āvī, -ātum, *wander, be mistaken (15)*

et (conj.), *and (2)*

evolō, -āre, -āvī, -ātum, *fly out of, fly away from (4)*

exitus, -ūs, m., *departure, outcome (11)*

exercitus, -ūs, m., *army (13)*

exspectō, -āre, -āvī, -ātum, *wait for, expect (4)*

et … et, *both … and (16)*

F

fābula, -ae, f., *story, legend (3)*

fabricō, -āre, -āvi, -ātum, *form, make, forge, shape (1)*

faciō, -ere, fēcī, factum, *make (9)*

famēs, famis, f., *hunger (8)*

fax, facis, f., *torch (2)*

fēmina, -ae, f., *woman (1)*

ferramentum, -ī, n., *iron tool (1)*

fidēs, fideī, f., *faith (14)*

fīlia, -ae, f., *daughter (8)*

fīlius, -ī, m., *son (5)*

flamma, -ae, f., *flame (2)*

flāvus, -a, -um, *yellow (12)*

fleō, -ēre, flēvī, flētum, *weep (4)*

floreō, -ēre, -uī, -------, *flourish, bloom (15)*

flōs, flōris, m., *flower (Rv. 15)*

fluctus, -ūs, m., *wave (of the sea) (13)*

fluō, fluere, fluxī, fluxum, *flow (8)*

flutō, -āre, -āvī, -ātum, *float (10)*

fluvius, -ī, m., *river (8)*

focus, -ī, m., *hearth, fireplace (16)*

folium, -ī, n., *leaf (7)*

fōns, fontis, m., *fountain (8)*

forma, -ae, f., *shape (3)*

frāter, frātris, m., *brother (3)*

fructus, -ūs, m., *fruit (11)*

frūmentum, -ī, n., *grain (plural—crops) (16)*

fugiō, -ere, fūgī, fugitum, *flee from (9)*

fulmen, fulminis, n., *thunderbolt, lightning (6)*

fugiō, -ere, fugī, fugitum, *flee from (9)*

fundus, -ī, m., *bottom, base (4)*

G

gaudium, -ī, n., *joy, happiness (10)*

gāvia, -ae, f., *seagull (9)*

genū, -ūs, n., *knee (12)*

gladius, -ī, m., *sword (Rv. 12)*

glēba, -ae, f., *dirt clod (7)*

Graecia, -ae, f., *Greece (Rv. 14)*

grāmen, grāminis, n., *grass (Rv. 15)*

grātus, -a, -um, *grateful, pleasing (16)*

H

habeō, -ēre, -uī, -itum, *have, hold (2)*

habēna, -ae, f., *strap, rein (6)*

habitō, -āre, -āvī, -ātum, *live in, inhabit (1)*

herba, -ae, f., *plant (15)*

herbōsus, -a, -um, *grassy (15)*

hērōs, hērōis, m., *hero (14)*

hiems, hiemis, f., *winter (6)*

hōra, -ae, f., *hour (Rv. 10)*

humus, -ī, f., *ground, earth, land (5)*

I

iaceō, -ēre, iacuī, ------, *lie (flat) (4)*

iactō, -āre, -āvī, -ātum, *throw (6)*

iecur, iecoris, n., *liver (2)*

ignis, ignis, m., *fire (1)*

impediō, -īre, -īvī, -ītum, *hinder (13)*

impetus, -ūs, m., *an attack (13)*

implōrō, -āre, -āvī, -ātum, *beg, implore (6)*

in (prep. with abl.), *in, on (2)*

incitō, -āre, -āvī, -ātum, *urge (16)*

inlaqueō, -āre, -āvī, -ātum, *entrap (Rv. 12)*

insula, -ae, f., *island (9)*

inter (prep. with acc.), *between, among (7)*

intra (prep. with acc.), *inside (4)*

inveniō, -īre, -vēnī, -ventum, *find, come upon (13)*

invidia, -ae, f., *envy (3)*

īra, -ae, f., *anger (2)*

īratus, -a, -um, *angry (16)*

iugulum, -ī, n., *throat (8)*

iugum, -ī, n., *a yoke (14)*

Iūlia, -ae, f., *Julia, sister of Julius (Rv. 1)*

Iūlius, -ī, m., *Julius (Rv. 1)*

Iuppiter, Iōvis, m., *Jupiter (Rv. 11)*

iuvō, -āre, iūvī, iūtum, *help (1)*

L

laborō, -āre, -āvī, -ātum, *work (Rv. 16)*

labyrinthus, -ī, m., *labyrinth (9)*

lāna, -ae, f., *wool (11)*

lapis, lapidis, m., *stone (8)*

laudō, -āre, -āvī, -ātum, *praise (Rv. 16)*

lavō, -āre, lāvī, lautum, *wash, bathe (Rv. 8)*

legō, -ere, lēgī, lectum, *gather, collect (Rv. 9)*

Glossary: Latin to English

levō, -āre, -avī, -ātum, *lift* (3)
liber, -brī, m, *book (Rv. 10)*
liberī, -ōrum, m., *children (Rv. 1)*
līberō, -āre, -āvī, -ātum, *set free, liberate (14)*
ligō, -āre, -āvī, -ātum, *tie or bind (2)*
līlium, -ī, n., *lily (15)*
līnea, -ae, f., *thread (10)*
liquefaciō, -facere, -fēcī, -factum, *melt (9)*
lītus, lītōris, n., *seashore (9)*
locus, -ī, m., *place (15)*
longus, -a -um, *long (Rv. 6)*
lūceō, -ēre, luxī, -----, *shine (5)*
lūcidus, -a, -um, *bright (5)*
lūcus, -ī, m., *grove (Rv. 14)*
ludus, -ī, m., *school, game (Rv. 10)*
lugeō, -ēre, luxī, ----------, *mourn (10)*
lūna, -ae, f., *moon (5)*

M magister, -trī, m., *master, teacher (Rv. 7)*
magnus, -a, -um, *large, great (Rv. 6)*
malevolentia, -ae, f., *spite, malice (3)*
mālum, -ī, n., *apple (Rv. 4)*
malum, -i, n., *an evil, a trouble (4)*
maneō, -ēre, mansī, mansum, *remain (10)*
manus, -ūs, f., *hand (11)*
mare, maris, n., *sea (9)*
marītus, -ī, m., *husband, bridegroom (4)*
māter, matris, f., mother (8)
memoria, -ae, f., *memory (16)*
mensa, -ae, f., *table (7)*
mensis, mensis, m., *month (6)*
meridiēs, -ēī, m., *noon (14)*
metus, -ūs, m., *fear (11)*
meus, mea, meum, *my (Rv. 15)*
mīles, mīlitis, m., *soldier (13)*
miser, misera, miserum, *wretched, miserable (8)*
misericordia, -ae, f., *pity, mercy (8)*
mittō, mittere, mīsī, missum, *send (16)*
moneō, -ēre, monuī, monitum, *warn (3)*
morbus, -ī, m., *sickness, disease (3)*
mors, mortis, f., *death (10)*

moveō, -ēre, movī, motum, *move (Rv. 2)*
multus, -a, -um, *much, many (Rv. 6)*
mundus, -ī, m., *world (5)*
muniō, -īre, -īvī, -ītum, *fortify, build (13)*
mūrus, -ī, m., *wall (Rv. 10)*
mūsica, -ae, f., *music (3)*
mutō, -āre, -āvī, -ātum, *change (12)*

N nam (conj.), *for (16)*
narrātor, narratōris, m., *storyteller (Rv. 5)*
narrō, -āre, -avī, -ātum *tell (Rv. 3)*
nauta, -ae, m., *sailor (13)*
nāvicula, -ae, f., *small boat (14)*
nāvigō, -āre, -avī, -ātum, *sail (13)*
nāvis, navis, f., *ship (13)*
neō, nēre, nēvī, nētum, *spin (11)*
nōn (adv.), *not (4)*
nōnus, -a, -um, *ninth (Rv. 6)*
noster, nostra, nostrum, *our (Rv. 15)*
nunc (adv.), *now (7)*
nuntiō, -āre, -āvī, -ātum, *announce (Rv. 12)*
nuntius, -ī, m., *messenger (14)*

O occultō, -āre, -āvī, -ātum, *hide (Rv. 8)*
octāvus, -a, -um, *eighth (Rv. 6)*
offerō, offere, obtulī, oblatum, *offer (8)*
offensa, -ae, f., *displeasure (12)*
operculum, -ī, n., *lid, cover (4)*
oppugnō, -āre, -āvī, -ātum, *attack (13)*
optātum, -ī, n., *a wish (6)*
optō, -āre, -āvī, -ātum, *wish for, desire, want (6)*
ornō, -āre, -āvī, -ātum, *equip, decorate (6)*
orō, -āre, -āvī, -ātum, *beg, ask for (16)*
ōs, ōris, n., *mouth (Rv. 15)*

P palla, -ae, f., *cloak (16)*
pānis, pānis, m., *bread (8)*
parō, -āre, -āvī, -ātum, *prepare (Rv. 7)*
parvus, -a, -um, *small (Rv. 6)*
pater, patris, m., *father (8)*
patria, -ae, f., *native land, country (5)*

patruus, -ī, m., *uncle (father's brother) (14)*

peccātum, -ī, n., *sin, error (12)*

per (prep. with acc.), *through (Rv. 9)*

periculōsus, -a, -um, *dangerous (5)*

perīculum, -ī, n., *danger (5)*

perītus, -a, -um, *skillful (11)*

perterritus, -a, -um, *frightened (16)*

perveniō, -īre, -vēnī, -ventum, *arrive, reach (13)*

Phaethōn, Phaethōnis, m., *son of Apollo (6)*

pila, -ae, f., *ball (Rv. 12)*

pinna, -ae, f., *feather (9)*

piscis, -is, m., *fish (Rv. 8)*

poena, -ae, f., *penalty, punishment (3)*

pomārium, -ī, n., *orchard (Rv. 7)*

pōmum, -ī, n., *fruit (15)*

pōnō, ponere, posuī, positum, *put, place (8)*

portō, -āre, -avī, -ātum *carry (Rv. 3)*

portus, -ūs, m., *harbor (13)*

pōtio, potiōnis, f., *potion (14)*

pōtō, -āre, -āvī, -ātum, *drink (7)*

possum, posse, potuī, -----, *be able (3)*

prātum, -ī, n., *meadow (15)*

prīmus, -a, -um, *first (Rv. 6)*

prope (prep. with acc.), *near (9)*

properō, -āre, -āvī, -ātum, *hasten, hurry (5)*

propter (prep. with acc.), *because of, on account of (12)*

prōvocō, -āre, -āvī, -ātum, *challenge (11)*

pugnō, -āre, -āvī, -ātum, *fight (Rv. 5)*

pulcher, pulchra, pulchrum, *beautiful, handsome (Rv. 6)*

purpureus, -a, -um, *purple (15)*

Q

quandō, *when (10)*

quartus, -a, -um, *fourth (Rv. 6)*

quid, *what (10)*

quintus, -a, -um, *fifth (Rv. 6)*

quīs, *who (10)*

quod (conj.), *because (2)*

quot, *how many (10)*

R

rāmulus, -ī, m., *twig (7)*

rāmus, -ī, m., *branch (7)*

raptō, -āre, -āvī, -ātum, *snatch, seize (16)*

rēgia, -ae, f., *palace (5)*

rēgīna, -ae, f., *queen (Rv. 5)*

regnum, -ī, n., *kingdom (13)*

regō, -ere, rēxī, rectum, *rule, govern (7)*

rēmigō, -āre, -āvī, -ātum, *row (13)*

rēmus, -ī, m., *oar (13)*

renovō, -āre, -āvi, -ātum, *renew (1)*

repente (adv.), *suddenly (4)*

rēs, reī, f., *thing, affair, matter (14)*

rēx, rēgis, m., *king (1)*

rīdeo, -ēre, rīsī, rīsum, *laugh, smile (Rv. 5)*

rogō, -āre, -āvī, -ātum, *ask (5)*

rōsa, -ae, f., *rose (7)*

ruber, rubra, rubrum, *red (12)*

S

sagittārius, -ī, m., *archer (6)*

sapientia, -ae, f., *wisdom (11)*

Saxum, -ī, n., *Saxum is a companion of the children (Rv. 1)*

saxum, -ī, n., *rock (1)*

scandō, -ere, scandī, scansum, *climb (9)*

scopulus, -ī, m., *cliff (Rv. 9)*

scorpius, -ī, m., *scorpion (6)*

secundus, -a, -um, *second (Rv. 6)*

sed (conj.), *but (2)*

sedeō, -ēre, sedī, sessum, *sit (2)*

senex, senis, m., *old man (8)*

septimus, -a, -um, *seventh (Rv. 6)*

sextus, -a, -um, *sixth (Rv. 6)*

silva, -ae, f., *forest (Rv. 15)*

simulō, -āre, -āvī, -ātum, *pretend (12)*

sol, solis, m., *sun (1)*

speciēs, -eī, f., *appearance (14)*

spectō, -āre, -āvī, -ātum, *watch, look at (Rv. 12)*

spēs, -eī, f., *hope (3)*

statim (adv.), *immediately (15)*

statua, -ae, f., *statue (8)*

stella, -ae, f., *star (5)*

stō, -āre, stetī, statum, *stand (5)*
stola, -ae, f., *dress (Rv. 9)*
stultus, -a, -um, *foolish (12)*
subitō (adv.), *suddenly (16)*
sum, esse, fuī, futūrum, *be (Rv. 11)*
superbia, -ae, f., *pride (12)*
superbus, -a, -um, *proud (Rv. 6)*
surgō, -ere, surrēxī, surrēctum, *rise, get up (7)*
suus, -a, -um, *his, her, its, their (15)*

T

tabula, -ae, f., *board (Rv. 10)*
tactiō, tactiōnis, f., *a touch (8)*
tangō, -ere, tetīgī, tactum, *touch (7)*
tardus, -a, -um, *slow (Rv. 6)*
taurus, -ī, m., *bull (6)*
tēla, -ae, f., *web, loom (12)*
tēlum, -ī, n., *weapon (2)*
templum, -ī, n., *temple (10)*
temptō, -āre, -āvī, -ātum, *try, attempt (4)*
terra, -ae, f., *land, earth (1)*
terreō, -ēre, terruī, territum, *frighten (4)*
tertius, -a, -um, *third (Rv. 6)*
texō, -ere, texuī, textum, *weave (11)*
textum, -ī, n., *cloth (11)*
trāns (prep. with acc.), *over, across (8)*
tum (adv.), *then (Rv. 7)*
turris, -is, f., *tower (9)*
tūtus, -a, -um, *safe (10)*
tuus, tua, tuum, *your (singular) (Rv. 15)*

U

ubi, *where (10)*
ululō, -āre, -āvī, -ātum, *howl, scream (Rv. 8)*
undique (adv.), *from all sides (15)*
usus, -ūs, m., *use, practice, experience (11)*
ūva, -ae, f., *grape (15)*
uxor, uxoris, f., *wife (4)*

V

vehementer (adv.), *exceedingly, very much (16)*
vellus, velleris, n., *fleece (14)*
veniō, -īre, vēnī, ventum, *come (13)*
ventus, -ī, m., *wind (Rv. 2)*
vēr, veris, n., *spring (6)*
verbum, -ī, n., *word (16)*
vēritās, vēritātis, f., *truth (Rv. 5)*
vestis, vestis, f., *clothing, garment (8)*
vester, vestra, vestrum, *your (plural) (Rv. 15)*
vetula, -ae, f., *old woman (12)*
videō, -ēre, vīdī, vīsum, *see (2)*
vigilō, -āre, -āvī, -ātum, *guard (Rv. 14)*
vīnea, -ae, f., *vineyard (Rv. 15)*
vīnum, -ī, n., *wine (7)*
vir, -ī, m., *man (1)*
virgō, virginis, f., *maiden (11)*
viridis, viride, *green (12)*
volō, -āre, -āvī, -ātum, *fly (9)*
vōx, vōcis, f., *voice (3)*
Vulcānus, -ī, m., *god of fire (6)*
vulturius, -ī, m., *vulture (2)*

G Glossary—English to Latin

The number in parentheses indicates the list in which the word is introduced. Some words from *Logos Latin 1, 2,* and *3* appear only in Review Lists. These words are indicated by the abbreviation *Rv.*.

A
about, *prep. w/abl., dē (3)*
across, *prep., w/acc., trāns (8)*
advice, *noun, cōnsilium, -ī, n. (12)*
Aesop, *noun, Aesōpus, Aesōpī, m. (Rv. 3)*
affair, *noun, rēs, reī, f. (14)*
(to) affix, *verb, adfīgō, adfīgere, adfīxī, adfīxum (9)*
against, *prep., w/abl, contrā (3)*
air, *noun, aer, aeris, m. (4)*
among, *prep., w/acc. inter (7)*
anchor, *noun, ancora, -ae, f. (14)*
and, *conj., et (2)*
anger, *noun, īra, -ae, f. (2)*
angry, *adj., īrātus, -a, -um (16)*
(to) announce, *verb, nuntiō, -āre, -āvī, -ātum (Rv. 12)*
another, *adj., alius, -a, -ud (15)*
appearance, *noun, speciēs, -eī, f. (14)*
apple, *noun, mālum, -ī, n. (Rv. 4)*
approach, *noun, adventus, -ūs, m. (11)*
archer, *noun, sagittārius, -ī, m. (6)*
arm, *noun, bracchium, -ī, n. (10)*
army, *noun, exercitus, -ūs, m. (13)*
around, *prep., w/acc., circā (10)*
arrival, *noun, adventus, -ūs, m. (11)*
(to) arrive, *verb, perveniō, -īre, -vēnī, -ventum (13)*
(to) ask, *verb, rogō, -āre, -āvī, -ātum (5)*
(to) ask for, *verb, orō, -āre, -āvī, -ātum (16)*
(to) assemble, *verb, conveniō, -īre, -vēnī, -ventum (13)*
(to) attach, *verb, adfīgō, -ere, -fīxī, -fīxum (Rv. 11)*

attack, *noun, impetus, -ūs, m. (13)*
(to) attack, *verb, oppugnō, -āre, -āvī, -ātum (13)*
(to) attempt, *verb, temptō, -āre, -āvī, -ātum (4)*
autumn, *noun, autumna, -ae, f. (6)*
Apollo, *noun, Apollō, Apollinis, m. (6)*
away from, *prep. w/acc., ā, ab (Rv. 2)*

B
ball, *noun, pīla, -ae, f. (Rv. 12)*
band of men, *noun, manus, -ūs, f. (Rv. 13)*
base, *noun, fundus, -ī, m. (4)*
(to) bathe, *verb, lavō, -āre, lāvī, lautum (Rv. 8)*
(to) be, *verb, sum, esse, fuī, futūrum (Rv. 11)*
(to) be able, *verb, possum, posse, potuī, ----- (3)*
beautiful, *adj., pulcher, pulchra, pulchrum (Rv. 6)*
because, *conj., quod (2)*
because of, *prep., w/acc., propter (12)*
(to) beg, *verb, implōrō, -āre, -āvī, -ātum (6)*
(to) beg, *verb, orō, -āre, -āvī, -ātum (16)*
between, *prep., w/acc. inter (7)*
(to) beware, *verb, caveō, -ēre, cāvī, cautum (4)*
(to) bind, *verb, ligō, -āre, -āvī, -ātum (2)*
bird, *noun, avis, -is, f. (9)*
(to) blaze, *verb, ardeō, -ēre, arsī, arsum (2)*
(to) bloom, *verb, floreō, -ēre, -uī, -------- (15)*
blue, *adj., caeruleus, -a, -um (12)*
(to) be mistaken, *verb, errō, -āre, -āvī, -ātum (15)*
board, *noun, tabula, -ae, f. (Rv. 10)*
body, *noun, corpus, corporis, n., (9)*
boldness, *noun, audācia, -ae, f. (Rv. 13)*
book, *noun, liber, -brī, m. (Rv. 10)*

both ... and, *conj., et ... et (16)*

bottom, *noun, fundus, -ī, m. (4)*

box, *noun, arca, -ae, f. (4)*

branch, *noun, rāmus, -ī, m. (7)*

bread, *noun, pānis, pānis, m. (8)*

bridegroom, *noun, marītus, -ī, m. (4)*

bright, *adj., lūcidus, -a, -um (5)*

(to) bring, *verb, apportō, -āre, -avī, -ātum (3)*

brother, *noun, frāter, frātris, m. (3)*

(to) build, *verb, aedificō, -āre, -āvī, -ātum (9)*

building, *noun, aedificium, -ī, n. (Rv. 9)*

bull, *noun, taurus, -ī, m. (6)*

(to) burn, *verb, ardeō, -ēre, arsī, arsum (2)*

but, *conj., sed (2)*

C **(to) capture,** *verb, capiō, -ere, cēpī, captum (9)*

care, *noun, cūra, -ae, f. (3)*

(to) carry, *verb, portō, -āre, -āvī, -ātum (Rv. 3)*

castle, *noun, castellum, -i, n., (Rv. 9)*

chariot, *noun, currus, -ūs, m. (2)*

chest, *noun, arca, -ae, f. (4)*

(to) challenge, *verb, prōvocō, -āre, -āvī, -ātum (11)*

(to) change, *verb, mutō, -āre, -āvī, -ātum (12)*

children, *verb, liberī, -ōrum, m. (Rv. 1)*

Claudius or Claude, *noun, Claudius, -ī, m. (Rv. 1)*

Claudia, *noun, Claudia, -ae, f. (Rv. 1)*

cliff, *noun, scopulus, -ī, m., (Rv. 9)*

(to) climb, *verb, scandō, -ere, scandī, scansum (9)*

cloak, *noun, palla, -ae, f. (16)*

cloth, *noun, textum, -ī, n. (11)*

clothing, *noun, vestis, vestis, f. (8)*

collect, *verb, legō, -ere, lēgī, lectum (Rv. 9)*

color, *noun, color, colōris, m. (12)*

come, *verb, veniō, -īre, vēnī, ventum (13)*

come upon, *verb, inveniō, -īre, -vēnī, -ventum (13)*

compete, *verb, contendō, -ere, contendī, contentum (11)*

concerning, *prep. w/abl., dē (3)*

constellation, *noun, astrum -ī, n. (5)*

(to) contend, *verb, contendō, -ere, contendī, contentum (11)*

country, *noun, patria, -ae, f. (5)*

cover, *noun, operculum, -ī, n. (4)*

(to) create, *verb, creō, -āre, -āvī, -ātum (1)*

crown, *noun, corōna, -ae, f. (14)*

D **danger,** *noun, periculum, -ī, n. (5)*

dangerous, *adj., perīculōsus, -a, -um (5)*

(to) dare, *verb, audeō, -ēre, ausus sum (11)*

daughter, *noun, filia, -ae, f. (8)*

day, *noun, diēs, diēī, m. (6)*

dear, *adj., cārus, -a, -um (15)*

death, *noun, mors, mortis, f. (10)*

(to) decorate, *verb, ornō, -āre, -āvī, -ātum (6)*

deep, *adj., altus, -a, -um (5)*

(to) defend, *verb, dēfendo, -ere, dēfendī, dēfēnsum (14)*

(to) delight, *verb, delectō, -āre, -āvī, -ātum (15)*

(to) demonstrate, *verb, dēmōnstrō, -āre, -āvī, -ātum (Rv. 11)*

departure, *noun, exitus, -ūs, m. (11)*

(to) desire, *verb, cupiō, cupere, cupīvī, cupītum (Rv. 15)*

(to) devour, *verb, dēvōrō, -āre, -āvi, -ātum (1)*

dinner, *noun, cēna, -ae, f. (7)*

dirt clod, *noun, glēba, -ae, f. (7)*

disease, *noun, morbus, -ī, m. (3)*

(to) desire, *verb, optō, -āre, -āvī, -ātum (6)*

displeasure, *noun, offensa, -ae, f. (12)*

divine, *adj., dīvīnus, -a, -um (16)*

dove, *noun, columba, -ae, f. (Rv. 14)*

down from, *prep. w/abl., dē (3)*

downfall, *noun, occāsus, -ūs, m. (12)*

dragon, *noun, dracō, dracōnis, m. (14)*

dress, *noun, stola, -ae, f. (Rv. 9)*

(to) drink, *verb, pōtō, -āre, -āvī, -ātum (7)*

(to) drive, *verb, agitō, -āre, -āvī, -ātum (2)*

(to) drop, *verb, cadō, -ere, cecīdī, casum (10)*

E **earth,** *noun, humus, -ī, f. (5)*

earth, *noun, terra, -ae, f. (1)*

(to) eat, *verb, edō, -ere, ēdī, ēsum (7)*

eighth, *adj., octāvus, -a, -um (Rv. 6)*

(to) entrap, *verb, inlaqueō, -āre, -āvī, -ātum (Rv. 12)*

envy, *noun, invidia, -ae, f. (3)*

(to) equip, *verb, ornō, -āre, -āvī, -ātum (6)*

error, *noun, peccātum, -ī, n. (12)*

evil, *noun, malum, -i, n. (4)*

exceedingly, *adv., vehementer (16)*

(to) expect, *verb, exspectō, -āre, -āvī, -ātum (4)*

experience, *noun, ūsus, -ūs, m. (11)*

F **faith,** *noun, fidēs, fideī, f. (14)*

(to) fall, *verb, cadō, -ere, cecīdī, casum (10)*

fast, *adj., citus, -a, -um (Rv. 6)*

(to) fasten to, *verb, adfīgō, adfigere, adfīxī, adfixum (9)*

father, *noun, pater, patris, m. (8)*

feather, *noun, pinna, -ae, f. (9)*

fear, *noun, metus, -ūs, m. (11)*

female friend, *noun, amīca, -ae, f. (Rv. 11)*

field, *noun, ager, agrī, m. (15)*

(to) fight, *verb, pugnō, -āre, -āvī, -ātum (Rv. 5)*

fifth, *adj., quīntus, -a, -um (Rv. 6)*

(to) fill, fill up, *verb, compleō, -ēre, complēvī, complētum (4)*

(to) find, *verb, inveniō, -īre, -vēnī, -ventum (13)*

fire, *noun, ignis, ignis, m. (1)*

fireplace, *noun, focus, -ī, m., (16)*

first, *adj., prīmus, -a, -um (Rv. 6)*

fish, *noun, piscis, -is, m. (Rv. 8)*

flame, *noun, flamma, -ae, f. (2)*

(to) flee from, *verb, fugiō, -ere, fūgī, fugitum (9)*

fleece, *noun, vellus, velleris, n. (14)*

(to) float, *verb, flutō, -āre, -āvī, -ātum (10)*

(to) flourish, *verb, floreō, -ēre, -uī, -------- (15)*

(to) flow, *verb, fluō, fluere, fluxī, fluxum (8)*

flower, *noun, flōs, flōris, m. (Rv. 15)*

(to) fly, *verb, volō, -āre, -āvī, -ātum (9)*

(to) fly away from, fly out of, *verb, evolō, -āre, -āvī, -ātum (4)*

food, *noun, cibus, -ī, m., (7)*

foolish, *adj., stultus, -a, -um (12)*

for, *conj., nam (16)*

for a long time, *adv., diū (Rv. 11)*

forest, *noun, silva, -ae, f. (Rv. 15)*

(to) forge, *verb, fabricō, -āre, -āvi, -ātum (1)*

(to) form, *verb, fabricō, -āre, -āvi, -ātum (1)*

fortify, *verb, muniō, -īre, -īvī, -ītum (13)*

fountain, *noun, fōns, fontis, m. (8)*

fourth, *adj., quartus, -a, -um (Rv. 6)*

friend, *noun, amīcus, -ī, m. (1)*

(to) frighten, *verb, terreō, -ēre, terruī, territum (4)*

frightened, *adj., perterritus, -a, -um (16)*

from, *prep. w/acc., ā, ab (Rv. 2)*

from, *prep. w/abl., dē (3)*

from, *prep., w/abl. ē, ex (Rv. 2)*

from all sides, *adv., undique (15)*

fruit, *noun, fructus, -ūs, m. (11)*

fruit, *noun, pōmum, -ī, n. (15)*

G **game,** *noun, ludus, -ī, m. (Rv. 10)*

garment, *noun, vestis, vestis, f. (8)*

(to) gather, *verb, legō, -ere, lēgī, lectum (Rv. 9)*

(to) get up, *verb, surgō, -ere, surrēxī, surrēctum (7)*

gift, *noun, dōnum, -ī, n. (2)*

(to) give, *verb, dō, -āre, dedī, datum (1)*

God, *noun, Deus, -ī, m. (1)*

goddess, *noun, dea, -ae, f. (11)*

gold, *noun, aurum, -ī, n. (5)*

golden, *adj., aureus, -a, -um (5)*

good, *adj., bonus, -a, -um (Rv. 6)*

goodwill, *noun, benevolentia, -ae, f. (3)*

govern, *verb, regō, -ere, rēxī, rectum (7)*

grain (plural—crops), *noun, frūmentum, -ī, n. (16)*

grandmother, *verb, avia, -ae, f. (Rv. 12)*

grape, *noun, ūva, -ae, f. (15)*

grass, *noun, grāmen, grāminis, n. (Rv. 15)*

grassy, *adj., herbōsus, -a, -um (15)*

grateful, *adj., grātus, -a, -um (16)*

Greece, *noun, Graecia, -ae, f. (Rv. 14)*

great, *adj., magnus, -a, -um (Rv. 6)*

greed, *noun, avāritia, -ae, f. (3)*

greedy, *adj., avārus, -a, -um (8)*

green, *adj., viridis, viride (12)*

(to) grieve, *verb, lūgeō, lūgēre, lūxī, ----- (Rv. 13)*

ground, *noun, humus, -ī, f. (5)*

grove, *noun, lūcus, -ī, m. (Rv. 14)*

(to) guard, *verb, vigilō, -āre, -āvī, -ātum (Rv. 14)*

(to) guard against, *verb, caveō, -ēre, cāvī, cautum (4)*

H

hair, *noun, coma, -ae, f. (Rv. 16)*

hair (often plural), *noun, capillus, -ī, m. (16)*

hand, *noun, manus, -ūs, f. (11)*

handsome, *adj., pulcher, pulchra, pulchrum (Rv. 6)*

happiness, *noun, gaudium, -ī, n. (10)*

harbor, *noun, portus, -ūs, m. (13)*

(to) hasten, *verb, properō, -āre, -āvī, -ātum (5)*

(to) have, *verb, habeō, -ēre, -uī, -itum (2)*

(to) hear, *verb, audio, -īre, -īvī, -ītum (13)*

hearth, *noun, focus, -ī, m., (16)*

heat, *calor, calōris, m. (10)*

heaven, *noun, caelum, -ī, n. (3)*

(to) help, *verb, iuvō, -āre, iūvī, iūtum (1)*

(to) hero, *noun, hērōs, hērōis, m. (14)*

(to) hide, *verb, occultō, -āre,-āvī, -ātum (Rv. 8)*

high, *adj., altus, -a, -um (5)*

hill, *noun, clīvus, -ī, m. (15)*

(to) hinder, *verb, impediō, -īre, -īvī, -ītum (13)*

his/her/its/their, *adj., suus, -a, -um (15)*

(to) hold, *verb, habeō, -ēre, -uī, -itum (2)*

home, *noun, domus, -ūs, f. (Rv. 5)*

hope, *noun, spēs, -eī, f. (3)*

horn (animal or trumpet), *noun, cornū, -ūs, n. (12)*

horse, *noun, equus, -ī, m. (2)*

hour, *noun, hōra, -ae, f. (Rv. 10)*

house, *noun, domus, -ūs, f. (Rv. 5)*

horse, *noun, equus, -ī, m. (Rv. 5)*

how many, *(indeclinable adj.) quot (10)*

(to) howl, *verb, ululō, -āre,-āvī, -ātum (Rv. 8)*

hunger, *noun, famēs, famis, f. (8)*

(to) hurry, *verb, properō, -āre, -āvī, -ātum (5)*

husband, *noun, marītus, -ī, m. (4)*

I

idea, *noun, cōgitātiō, cōgitatiōnis, f. (9)*

immediately, *adv., statim (15)*

(to) implore, *verb, implōrō, -āre, -āvī, -ātum (6)*

in, *prep. w/abl. in (2)*

(to) inhabit, *verb, habitō, -āre, -āvi, -ātum (1)*

insect, *bēstiola, -ae, f. (Rv. 12)*

inside, *prep., w/acc. intrā (4)*

iron tool, *noun, ferramentum, -ī, n. (1)*

island, *noun, insula, -ae, f. (9)*

J

joy, *noun, gaudium, -ī, n. (10)*

Julia, *noun, Iūlia, -ae, f. (Rv. 1)*

Julius, *noun, Iūlius, -ī, m. (Rv. 1)*

Jupiter, *noun, Iuppiter, Iōvis, m., (Rv. 11)*

K

kindness, *noun, benevolentia, -ae, f. (3)*

king, *noun, rēx, rēgis, m. (1)*

kingdom, *noun, rēgnum, -ī, n. (13)*

knee, *noun, genū, -ūs, n. (12)*

L

labyrinth, *noun, labyrinthus, -ī, m. (9)*

land, *noun, humus, -ī, f. (5)*

land, *noun, terra, -ae, f. (1)*

large, *adj., magnus, -a, -um (Rv. 6)*

(to) laugh, *verb, rīdeo, -ēre, rīsī, rīsum (Rv. 5)*

(to) lead, *verb, dūcō, -ere, dūxī, ductum (7)*

leaf, *noun, folīum, -ī, n. (7)*

leaves of a tree, *noun, coma, -ae, f. (Rv. 16)*

legend, *noun, fābula, -ae, f. (3)*

(to) liberate, *verb, līberō, -āre, -āvī, -ātum (14)*

lid, *noun, operculum, -ī, n. (4)*

(to) lie (flat), *verb, iaceō, -ēre, iacuī, ------ (4)*

(to) lift, *verb, levō, -āre, -avī, -ātum (3)*

lightning, *noun, fulmen, fulminis, n. (6)*

(to) like, *verb, amō, -āre, -āvi, -ātum (1)*

lily, *noun, līlium, -ī, n. (15)*

line of battle, *noun, aciēs, acieī, f. (14)*

(to) listen to, *verb, auscultō, -āre, -āvī, -ātum (Rv. 3)*

(to) live in, *verb, habitō, -āre, -āvi, -ātum (1)*

liver, *noun, iecur, iecoris, n. (2)*

long, *adj., longus, -a -um (Rv. 6)*

loom, *noun, tēla, -ae, f., (12)*

(to) love, *verb, amō, -āre, -āvi, -ātum (1)*

M   **maiden,** *noun, virgō, virginis, f. (11)*

(to) make, *verb, fabricō, -āre, -āvi, -ātum (1)*

(to) make, *verb, faciō, -ere, fēcī, factum (9)*

male friend, *noun, amīcus, -ī, m. (Rv. 11)*

malice, *noun, malevolentia, -ae, f. (3)*

man, *noun, vir, -ī, m. (1)*

many, *adj., multus, -a, -um (Rv. 6)*

master, *noun, magister, -trī, m. (Rv. 7)*

matter, *noun, rēs, reī, f. (14)*

meadow, *noun, prātum, -ī, n. (15)*

meal, *noun, cēna, -ae, f. (7)*

(to) melt, *verb, liquefaciō, -facere, -fēcī, -factum (9)*

memory, *noun, memoria, -ae, f. (16)*

mercy, *noun, misericordia, -ae, f. (8)*

messenger, *noun, nuntius, -ī, m. (14)*

miserable, *adj., miser, misera, miserum (8)*

(to) miss, *verb, desiderō, -āre, -āvī, -ātum (15)*

month, *noun, mensis, mensis, m. (6)*

moon, *noun, lūna, -ae, f. (5)*

mother, *noun, māter, mātris, f. (8)*

(to) mourn, *verb, lūgeō, -ēre, lūxī, ---------- (10)*

mouth, *noun, ōs, ōris, n. (Rv. 15)*

(to) move, *verb, moveō, -ere, mōvī, mōtum (Rv. 2)*

much, *adj., multus, -a, -um (Rv. 6)*

music, *noun, mūsica, -ae, f. (3)*

my, *adj., meus, mea, meum (Rv. 15)*

N   **native land,** *noun, patria, -ae, f. (5)*

near, *prep., w/acc., prope (9)*

ninth, *adj., nōnus, -a, -um (Rv. 6)*

needle, *noun, acus, -ūs, f. (11)*

noon, *noun, meridiēs, -ēī, m. (14)*

not, *adverb, nōn (4)*

now, *adv., nunc (7)*

O   **oar,** *noun, rēmus, -ī, m. (13)*

(to) offer, *verb, offerō, offere, obtulī, oblātum (8)*

old man, *noun, senex, senis, m., (8)*

old woman, *noun, vetula, -ae, f. (12)*

on, *prep. w/abl. in (2)*

on account of, *prep., w/acc., propter (12)*

orchard, *noun, pomārium, -ī, n. (Rv. 7)*

other, *adj., alius, -a, -ud (15)*

our, *adj., noster, nostra, nostrum (Rv. 15)*

out of, *prep., w/abl. ē, ex (Rv. 2)*

outcome, *noun, exitus, -ūs, m. (11)*

over, *prep., w/acc., trāns (8)*

P   **palace,** *noun, rēgia, -ae, f. (5)*

penalty, *noun, poena, -ae, f. (3)*

Phaeton, *noun, Phaethōn, Phaethōnis, m. (6)*

pity, *noun, misericordia, -ae, f. (8)*

place, *noun, locus, -ī, m. (15)*

(to) place, *verb, pōnō, ponere, posuī, positum (8)*

plain, *noun, campus, -ī, m. (15)*

(to) place, *verb, pōnō, ponere, posuī, positum (Rv. 15)*

plan, *noun, cōnsilium, -ī, n. (12)*

plant, *noun, herba, -ae, f. (15)*

(to) play (on an instrument), *verb, w/abl., canō, -ere, cecinī, cantum (Rv. 12)*

pleasing, *adj., grātus, -a, -um (16)*

(to) plow, *verb, arō, -āre, -āvī, -ātum (1)*

(to) pluck, *verb, carpō, -ere, carpsī, carptum (7)*

(to) point out, *verb, dēmōnstrō, -āre, -āvī, -ātum (1)*

potion, *noun, pōtio, potiōnis, f. (14)*

practice, *noun, ūsus, -ūs, m. (11)*

(to) praise, *verb, laudō, -āre, -āvī, -ātum (Rv. 16)*

(to) prepare, *verb, parō, -āre, -āvī, -ātum (Rv. 7)*

(to) pretend, *verb, simulō, -āre, -āvī, -ātum (12)*

pride, *noun, superbia, -ae, f. (12)*

prison, *noun, carcer, carceris, m. (9)*

proud, *adj., superbus, -a, -um (Rv. 6)*

punishment, *noun, poena, -ae, f. (3)*

purple, *adj., purpureus, -a, -um (15)*

(to) put, *verb, pōnō, ponere, posuī, positum (8)*

Q   queen, *noun, rēgīna, -ae, f. (Rv. 5)*

R   ram, *noun, ariēs, ariētis, m. (14)*

(to) recognize, *verb, cōgnoscō, -ere, cōgnōvī, cōgnitum (7)*

(to) reach, *verb, perveniō, -īre, -vēnī, -ventum (13)*

red, *adj., ruber, rubra, rubrum (12)*

(to) rein, *verb, habēna, -ae, f. (6)*

(to) remain, *verb, maneō, -ēre, mansī, mansum (10)*

(to) renew, *verb, renovō, -āre, -āvi, -ātum (1)*

(the) rest (of), *adj., cēterī, -ae, -a (16)*

(to) rise, *verb, surgō, -ere, surrēxī, surrēctum (7)*

(to) rise up, *verb, surgō, surgere, surrēxī, surrēctum (Rv. 16)*

river, *verb, fluvius, -ī, m. (8)*

rock, *noun, saxum, -ī, n. (1)*

rose, *noun, rōsa, -ae, f. (7)*

(to) row, *verb, rēmigō, -āre, -āvī, -ātum (13)*

(to) rule, *verb, regō, -ere, rēxī, rectum (7)*

(to) run, *verb, currō, -ere, cucurrī, cursum (Rv. 8)*

S   safe, *adj., tūtus, -a, -um (10)*

(to) sail, *verb, navigō, -āre, -āvi, -ātum (13)*

sailor, *noun, nauta, -ae, m. (13)*

Saxum, *noun, Saxum, -ī, n. (Rv. 1)*

(to) say, *verb, dīcō, -ere, dīxī, dictum (7)*

school, *noun, ludus, -ī, m. (Rv. 10)*

scorpion, *noun, scorpius, -ī, m. (6)*

(to) scream, *verb, ululō, -āre,-āvī, -ātum (Rv. 8)*

sea, *noun, mare, maris, n. (9)*

seashore, *noun, lītus, litōris, n. (Rv. 13)*

seagull, *noun, gāvia, -ae, f. (9)*

seashore, *noun, lītus, litōris, n. (9)*

second, *adj., secundus, -a, -um (Rv. 6)*

(to) see, *verb, videō, -ēre, vīdī, vīsum (2)*

(to) seize, *verb, raptō, -āre, -āvī, -ātum (16)*

(to) send, *verb, mitto, mittere, mīsī, missum (16)*

(to) set free, *verb, līberō, -āre, -āvī, -ātum (14)*

seventh, *adj., septimus, -a, -um (Rv. 6)*

(to) shut in, *verb, arceō, -ēre, arcuī, --------- (4)* sickness, *verb, morbus, -ī, m. (3)*

silver, *noun, argentum, -ī, n. (5)*

silver, silvery, *adj. argenteus, -a, -um (5)*

shape, *noun, forma, -ae, f. (3)*

(to) shape, *verb, fabricō, -āre, -āvī, -ātum (Rv. 9)*

sharp, *adj., acutūs, -a, -um (11)*

(to) shine, *verb, lūceō, -ēre, lūxī, ----- (5)*

ship, *noun, nāvis, nāvis, f. (13)*

(to) shout, *verb, clamō, -āre, -āvī, -ātum (10)*

(to) show, *verb, dēmōnstrō, -āre, -āvī, -ātum (1)*

sick, *aeger, aegra, aegrum (Rv. 10)*

sin, *noun, peccātum, -ī, n. (12)*

(to) sit, *verb, sedeō, -ēre, sēdī, sessum (2)*

sixth, *adj., sextus, -a, -um (Rv. 6)*

skill, *noun, ars, artis, f. (11)*

skillful, *adj., perītus, -a, -um (11)*

sky, *noun, caelum, -ī, n. (3)*

(to) sleep, *verb, dormiō, -īre, -īvī, -ītum (13)*

slow, *adj., tardus, -a, -um (Rv. 6)*

small, *adj., parvus, -a, -um (Rv. 6)*

small boat, *noun, nāvicula, -ae, f. (14)*

(to) smile, *verb, rīdeō, -ēre, rīsī, rīsum (Rv. 5)*

(to) snatch, *verb, raptō, -āre, -āvī, -ātum (16)*

soldier, *noun, mīles, mīlitis, m. (13)*

son, *noun, fīlius, -ī, m. (5)*

(to) speak, *verb, dīcō, -ere, dīxī, dictum (7)*

speed, *noun, celeritās, celeritātis, f. (12)*

spider, *noun, arānea, -ae, f. (12)*

(to) spin, *verb, neō, nēre, nēvī, nētum (11)*

spite, *noun, malevolentia, -ae, f. (3)*

spring, *noun, vēr, vēris, n. (6)*

(to) stand, *verb, stō, -āre, stetī, statum (5)*

star, *noun, stella, -ae, f. (5)*

statue, *noun, statua, -ae, f. (8)*

stone, *noun, lapis, lapidis, m. (8)*

story, *noun, fābula, -ae, f. (3)*

storyteller, *noun, narrātor, narratōris, m. (Rv. 5)*

straight line, *noun, aciēs, acieī, f. (14)*

strap, *noun, habēna, -ae, f. (6)*

star, *noun, stella, -ae, f. (Rv. 16)*
suddenly, *adv., repente (4)*
suddenly, *adv., subitō (16)*
summer, *noun, aestās, aestātis, f. (6)*
sun, *noun, sōl, sōlis, m. (1)*
(to) swallow, *verb, dēvōrō, -āre, -āvi, -ātum (1)*
swift, *adj., citus, -a, -um (Rv. 6)*
sword, *noun, gladius, -ī, m. (Rv. 12)*

table, *noun, mensa, -ae, f. (7)*
tall, *adj., altus, -a, -um (Rv. 10)*
(to) teach, *verb, doceō, -ēre, docuī, doctum (10)*
teacher, *noun, magister, -trī, m. (Rv. 7)*
(to) tell, *verb, dīcō, -ere, dīxī, dictum (7)*
(to) tell, *verb, narrō, -āre, -āvī, -ātum (Rv. 3)*
temple, *noun, templum, -ī, n. (10)*
tenth, *adj., decimus, -a, -um (Rv. 6)*
(to) tie, *verb, ligō, -āre, -āvī, -ātum (2)*
then, *adv., tum (Rv. 7)*
thing, *noun, rēs, reī, f. (14)*
third, *adj., tertius, -a, -um, (Rv. 6)*
thread, *noun, līnea, -ae, f. (10)*
throat, *noun, iugulum, -ī, n. (8)*
through, *prep., w/acc., per (Rv. 9)*
(to) throw, *verb, iactō, -āre, -āvī, -ātum (6)*
thunderbolt, *noun, fulmen, fulminis, n. (6)*
tired, *adj., dēfessus, -a, -um (Rv. 6)*
tooth, *noun, dens, dentis, m. (14)*
touch, *noun, tactiō, tactiōnis, f. (8)*
tower, *noun, turris, -is, f., (9)*
tree, *noun, arbor, arboris, f. (Rv. 7)*
trouble, *noun, malum, -ī, n. (4)*
truth, *noun, vēritās, vēritātis, f. (Rv. 5)*
(to) try, *verb, temptō, -āre, -āvī, -ātum (4)*
to, *prep. w/acc., ad (2)*
torch, *noun, fax, facis, f. (2)*
touch, *verb, tangō, -ere, tetīgī, tactum (7)*
toward, *prep. w/acc., ad (2)*
twig, *noun, rāmulus, -ī, m. (7)*
uncle (father's brother), *noun, patruus, -ī, m. (14)*

uncle (mother's brother), *adj., avunculus, -ī, m. (Rv. 14)*
(to) urge, *verb, incitō, -āre, -āvī, -ātum (16)*
use, *noun, ūsus, -ūs, m. (11)*

very much, *adv., vehementer (16)*
vineyard, *noun, vīnea, -ae, f. (Rv. 15)*
voice, *noun, vōx, vōcis, f. (3)*
Vulcan, *Vulcānus, -ī, m. (6)*
vulture, *noun, vulturius, -ī, m. (2)*

(to) wait for, *verb, exspectō, -āre, -āvī, -ātum (4)*
(to) walk, *verb, ambulō, -āre, -āvī, -ātum (Rv. 2)*
wall, *noun, mūrus, -ī, m. (Rv. 10)*
(to) wander, *verb, errō, -āre, -āvī, -ātum (15)*
(to) want, *verb, cupiō, cupere, cupīvī, cupītum (Rv. 15)*
(to) want, *verb, desiderō, -āre, -āvī, -ātum (15)*
(to) want, *verb, optō, -āre, -āvī, -ātum (6)*
(to) warn, *verb, moneō, -ēre, monuī, monitum (3)*
(to) wash, *verb, lavō, -āre, lāvī, lautum (Rv. 8)*
water, *noun, aqua, -ae, f. (Rv. 8)*
wave (of the sea), *noun, fluctus, -ūs, m. (13)*
wax, *noun, cēra, -ae, f. (10)*
weapon, *noun, telum, -ī, n. (2)*
(to) weave, *verb, texō, -ere, texuī, textum (11)*
web, *noun, tēla, -ae, f., (12)*
(to) weep, *verb, fleō, -ēre, flēvī, flētum (4)*
what, *quid (10)*
when, *quandō (10)*
where, *adv., ubi (10)*
while, *adv., dum (Rv. 15)*
white, *adj., albus, -a, -um (Rv. 6)*
who, *quis (10)*
wife, *noun, uxor, uxoris, f. (4)*
wind, *noun, ventus, -ī, m. (Rv. 2)*
wine, *noun, vīnum, -ī, n. (7)*
wing, *noun, ala, -ae, f. (4)*
winter, *noun, hiems, hiemis, f. (6)*
wisdom, *noun, sapientia, -ae, f. (11)*
wish, *noun, optātum, -ī, n. (6)*

(to) wish, *verb, cupiō, cupere, cupīvī, cupītum (Rv. 15)*

(to) wish for, *verb, optō, -āre, -āvī, -ātum (6)*

woman, *noun, fēmina, -ae, f. (1)*

wool, *verb, lāna, -ae, f. (11)*

word, *noun, verbum, -ī, n. (16)*

world, *noun, mundus, -ī, m. (5)*

(to) work, *verb, laborō, -āre, -āvī, -ātum (Rv. 16)*

worry, *noun, cūra, -ae, f. (3)*

(to) worship, *verb, adōrō, -āre, -āvī, -ātum (16)*

wretched, *adj., miser, misera, miserum (8)*

Y

year, *noun, annus, -ī, m. (6)*

yellow, *adj., flāvus, -a, -um (12)*

yoke, *iugum, -ī, n. (14)*

young man, *noun, adulēscēns, adulēscentis, m. (14)*

your (plural), *adj., vester, vestra, vestrum (Rv. 15)*

your (singular), *adj., tuus, tua, tuum (Rv. 15)*

Glossary: English to Latin

Ⓘ Index